A Priest's Life

THE CALLING, THE COST, THE JOY

A Priest's Life

THE CALLING, THE COST, THE JOY

PREFACE BY

ARCHBISHOP EDWIN F. O'BRIEN

Compiled and edited by Patricia Mitchell

theWORD among us® press

14 13 12 11 10 1 2 3 4 5

ISBN: 978-1-59325-168-0

Cover design by Jason Gabbert, Faceout Studio, faceoutsudio.com

Made and printed in the United States of America

Library of Congress Control Number: 2009944199

Contents

CONTENTS

Preface

"The priesthood is the love of the heart of Jesus."
—*St. John Mary Vianney*

We all live busy lives—priests and laypeople alike—and sometimes we fail to take the time to truly reflect on what we do and why we do it. Inspired, no doubt, by the Holy Spirit, Pope Benedict XVI in June 2009 inaugurated a Year for Priests. He was wise to do so, for it has given all of us in the Church time to meditate on the great gift of the priesthood.

What makes a great priest? When he announced the Year for Priests, Pope Benedict declared St. John Vianney the universal patron of priests and relied on him as the model for all priests. What was it about this nineteenth-century French pastor—a simple parish priest who ministered in the small village of Ars—that warrants such an honor? Here are some of the pope's observations about John Vianney's ministry:

- He identified himself completely with his ministry. There is "extraordinary fruitfulness," the pope said, when the holiness of the ministry of the priesthood coincides with the holiness of the person who is the priest.

- He taught his parishioners primarily by the witness of his life. It was from his example that they learned to pray. He communicated the presence of Jesus in the Eucharist to his parishioners by the way he celebrated Mass.

- He was convinced that the fervor of a priest's life depended entirely on the Mass, and when he celebrated, he offered up his own life in sacrifice.

- He put his "unfailing trust" in the Sacrament of Reconciliation, and made it the center of his pastoral concerns.

- He practiced the evangelical counsels of poverty, chastity, and obedience, even though they were not required of him as a diocesan priest.

In his letter, Pope Benedict noted that throughout his life, St. John Vianney remained in awe of the gift and task entrusted to human beings through the priesthood. And what a great gift it is! As I recently told a group of retired priests in my archdiocese, if the Blessed Mother herself were to appear in our midst today, she could not do what the simplest priest does every day and what she did physically in Bethlehem: give us the Sacrament of the Body and Blood of Christ. Nor could all the angels and archangels in heaven, acting in full unison, forgive even one venial sin. Only the priest, acting in the person of Christ, can do these things and so much more, not of his own merits or power, but because he is chosen, called, and empowered by God himself to continue the saving work of the risen Jesus.

No human being can ever feel worthy of such a gift—or such a responsibility. Because we are human, there will be times when we fail. But our response to our weaknesses must be to cling ever more closely to Christ. To be good and holy priests, we need a fervent prayer life, the sacraments, and immersion in God's word. Pope Benedict's letter proclaiming the Year for Priests ends by urging priests to make a commitment "to the ideal of complete self-oblation to Christ and the Church, which inspired the thoughts and actions of the saintly Curé of Ars."

For me, *A Priest's Life: The Calling, the Cost, the Joy* captures that idea of "self-oblation"—that gift of self—spoken of by the Holy Father. Some of the priests in this book speak of their initial gift of self to Jesus and his Church in their discernment leading up to ordination. Others speak of the ongoing need to offer themselves to Jesus, as they identify with Christ as "a living sacrifice" (Romans 12:1). All these stories show both the joy and the sacrifice of this vocation.

The Word Among Us has done a service for the Church in collecting and publishing these stories. They reflect the many and varied ways priests are serving the Church throughout the world. They also provide us with a glimpse into the hearts of these priests—what moves them, what energizes them, and what fulfills them. Above all, these stories help us to see more clearly why the priesthood is such a gift to the Church, and why we need to continue praying for our priests and asking God for more priestly vocations.

I would like to invite readers of this book to pray for priests in a special way. As you intercede for them, ask the Lord to keep all priests close to his heart and renew in them the passion that they need to carry out their duties faithfully each day.

My motto as archbishop is taken from Jeremiah 3:15: *I will give you shepherds.* God has promised to give us priestly vocations, but we also need to be faithful in praying for them. I have noticed that in those parishes and dioceses where there is an abundance of Eucharistic adoration, there is an abundance of priestly vocations. They have taken seriously the Lord's solution for great harvests but too few laborers: "Pray the harvest master to send laborers into his harvest" (see Matthew 9:38). Let us all take up this practice regularly and ask the Lord to send us priests for his Church.

We are blessed, indeed, to have many deacons, religious, and lay people working the harvest. But without the priest, there is no Eucharist. And without the Eucharist, there is no Church. How fitting, then, and how necessary, to turn to the Eucharist in our prayer for priests, especially in this Year for Priests.

Most Rev. Edwin F. O'Brien
Archbishop of Baltimore

Introduction

When Pope Benedict XVI inaugurated a Year for Priests in June 2009, he did it first and foremost for the priests themselves. He invited them to renew their faith so that they could become ever more effective witnesses to the gospel in the world today.

But this Year for Priests is for the whole Church as well. Not only does it help those of us in the laity to take a step back and recall the vital role of the priest in the Church and in our faith lives, it also inspires us to encourage and pray for all of our priests. At The Word Among Us, we thought that one way we could celebrate this special Year is to publish *A Priest's Life: The Calling, the Cost, the Joy*.

In these times, when we often hear about the weaknesses and failings of priests, we wanted to compile these stories and witnesses to honor the many thousands of priests worldwide who serve us so selflessly. The priests you will meet in these pages are hardly representative of all the priests serving the Church today. And yet, in another sense, they are. As you read their stories, you will see beyond the specific circumstances of their lives to the passion they have to serve God in this special way. They love the Lord, they love the people they serve, and they love this vocation that God has given to them.

A Priest's Life features stories of priests serving God in many different ways—in parishes, in foreign missions, as prison chaplains, as teachers and preachers, on battlefields. Some of the men in this book write about their path to becoming priests—the discernment, the challenges, and finally the certainty that they are doing what God wants for them. Others write about their ministries. Some have traveled the globe as evangelists, proclaiming the good news. Others are parish priests who faithfully, day in and day out, carry out their duties and often discover, much to their surprise, that they have been the catalyst to a changed life. Some of these stories relate a powerful moment in the ministry of that priest, such as caring for survivors of 9/11, praying with a person who is then healed, or hearing the confession of a person who has spent a lifetime away from the Church.

Though their ministries, their paths, and their years of service differ, these men share a common calling from God to serve him in the priesthood, and they all reflect the joy and fulfillment of living out that call. Whatever their story, all the priests who contributed to this book convey an energy and excitement about their lives, and in so doing, they honor every priest who seeks to live for the Lord and serve his Church. We hope that these stories will move you in one way or another, just as they have moved us. We are indebted to those who have taken time from their very busy schedules to write them.

Our Church needs priests who, like all of us, can find the time to nurture their own relationship with the Lord while at the same time serving others. It is only with the Lord's power and grace that any of us can begin to live up to our vocations. We all need to support one another as we strive to live out the great calling that God has given to each of us in baptism.

In this Year for Priests and beyond, may we all remember to pray for our priests each day. May we remember to thank them for the work they do. May we encourage them with our love and support. May we also ask the Lord to shower his grace on men who are discerning a call to the priesthood. We, the Church, need priests.

Lord, send us men whose hearts are enflamed with your love so that they are willing to become a living sacrifice for you. We thank you for the priests that serve us so faithfully today. Renew their hearts—and ours as well—so that together we can love and serve your body on earth.

Jeff Smith
President
The Word Among Us, Inc.

Patricia Mitchell
Editorial Director
The Word Among Us Press

The People's Prayer for Priests

The U.S. Conference of Catholic Bishops has recommended that parishes offer this prayer throughout the Year for Priests.

Dear Lord,
> We pray that the Blessed Mother
> wrap her mantle around your priests
> and through her intercession
> strengthen them for their ministry.

We pray that Mary will guide your priests
> to follow her own words,
>> "Do whatever He tells you" (John 2:5).

May your priests have the heart of St. Joseph,
> Mary's most chaste spouse.

May the Blessed Mother's own pierced heart
> inspire them to embrace
> all who suffer at the foot of the cross.

May your priests be holy,
> filled with the fire of your love,
> seeking nothing but your greater glory
> and the salvation of souls.

Amen.

Saint John Vianney, pray for us.

Chapter 1

Why Did I Fear?

Fr. Gerard Francik

Sometimes it's not clear to us what God's call is in our lives. It can seem very mysterious. But what I've witnessed again and again, especially in my work now as vocation director for our diocese, is that if we believe that God is calling us and we respond in faith, he will confirm that call with a sense of his joy, presence, and peace. That has certainly been the case in my own life.

God spoke very clearly to me one morning as I was walking across my college campus. I had been in one major freshman year, and then had changed to another—mass communications. (Funny that God used that in a different way!) I enjoyed my classes, was getting good grades, and had completed several internships.

But something was missing. I just couldn't imagine myself working in this field every day from nine to five. I thought that after a few years, I would get bored. So what should I do? That day God spoke very clearly in my mind. No lightning bolts or thundering voices from mountaintops, just a clear thought: "Be a priest." Of course I ran away from the idea, thinking it was the strangest thing in the world. But looking back, I can see what had contributed to this "idea."

A newly ordained priest had just arrived the year before in my parish. His life looked great. People loved him; he loved the liturgy and the people. In him I saw a bit of myself. I had always loved the liturgy, music, and my faith, but with his encouragement, I became directly involved in the parish. I joined the liturgy committee and helped with music, the youth group, and the RCIA program. My faith blossomed, and I felt God's call, which was accompanied by a sense of joy and peace. When I was involved in church, I was at home. When I finally entered the seminary three years later, I woke up late one night and asked myself, "Why did I fear?" God's presence and confirmation were so real.

Making a Difference

I want to share with you two stories that show why I am a priest and how God continues to confirm his calling to me. Just a few months ago, I received a phone call from a young woman who now lived .on the West Coast. She was going to be in town for a few days and wanted to stop by and visit with me. I had no idea why. I didn't even recognize her name, but there I was, a few days later, greeting her and her mother at the door.

She came into my office, and with tears in her eyes recounted the story of the death of her stepfather. Neither she nor her mother had been Catholic, but they remembered my taking care of her father when he was hospitalized and later as he was dying. She said that I had included them so much in the funeral, even though they did not understand all of the rituals. She wanted me to know how grateful she was. I thought that was the end of the conversation.

But then she described how, days later, she and her boyfriend were driving in a car together and had a terrible accident. He was killed. Others blamed her for his death, and in fact, she found herself feeling terribly guilty (even though she was not) and blaming herself. One desperate day, driving through some country roads at very high speeds, she decided to try to find me. I had been transferred to our youth retreat house. Luckily, after she checked with the front office, I appeared and was able to sit and talk with her. She said it took no more than five minutes, but that conversation changed her life. She left there feeling God's presence and peace.

That young woman came back to thank me. She said she thought that priests too frequently are not told how they have helped another in need. I honestly don't remember the conversation that she said changed her life.

Five years ago a couple I married called with great news. I knew that they had wanted children and that, for years, they were unable to conceive. This time the news was different: They were going to have a baby. They had heard from an adoption agency, and they were flying to China to meet their new little girl. They would be there two weeks but wanted to arrange for her baptism when they returned. "Would you be willing to baptize our baby?" the husband asked. "Of course," I replied. "I would be honored." I then asked how his parents must feel, since he was an only child and this would be their first grandchild. He said, "Oh, we haven't told them yet. We wanted to tell you first!" I was speechless. One of the most poignant and important moments of life, and they wanted me to be part of it first.

That is why I am still a priest. I am able to walk into the most profound moments in people's lives and make a difference. God confirms his call to me every day by using me to bring his blessings and grace to others in so many ways. Most of the time, I'm not even aware that he is using me, because it is God giving the blessings and grace, not me. And people like these, who cross my path every day, are such a blessing to me personally. Is life as a priest lonely? Not with wonderful people like these!

Fr. Gerard Francik was born in Baltimore in 1960 and graduated from Towson University before entering the seminary in 1982. He was ordained a priest for the Archdiocese of Baltimore on May 16, 1987 and is currently serving as vocation director for the archdiocese.

Chapter 2

The Thrill of Proclaiming the Good News

Fr. Tom Forrest, CSsR

A number of times I've begun a talk by lifting my arms and shouting out joyfully: "I want you all to know that I am a very happy man!" Whenever I've performed this little dramatization, those in the audience have responded with applause, giving the impression that it was rare for them to hear someone say that they were living a very enjoyable life.

I said this, though, only because it was—and remains—true. I've been a priest now for fifty-five years, and every one of those years has been joyful and satisfying, and I hope fruitful as well. I've done some difficult priestly jobs, and for a time faced a persecution that could have cost me my life. But though I've never had the comforts of a wife and children of my own, or worldly fame and fortune, I would never willingly trade my life for that of any great ballplayer, movie star, or corporate CEO.

The first five or six years of my early childhood were not unique in any way. The most I can say is that they happened just as God wanted them to happen, and in ways that were blessings for me. Like most young boys, my first ambition was to become either a policeman or fireman. Such hopes lingered until the Sunday of my First Holy Communion, and from then on and forever since, my sole desire was to be a priest—hopefully a good one. The dream, though, was never to become the parish priest just down the street. No, from the beginning my ambition was to serve as a missionary priest, hopefully "somewhere in deepest Africa."

That dream of living and ministering in an African village may have come from the *Tarzan of the Apes* books and films that fascinated me so much in my boyhood years. At the same time, the thoughts of priesthood were inspired by a young parish priest by the name of Fr. Fey, who for some reason knew me by name and always greeted me in the nicest way.

Because there was not as yet a Catholic school in my neighborhood, I began my early education in a public school. One day our sixth-grade teacher invited her students to express their hopes for a future career. The replies were predictable—policeman or fireman, teacher or nurse—until it was my turn. "Priest," I said. My classmates laughed out loud, and with good reason. In those early years, I didn't exactly glow with sanctity and spirituality. But the good teacher quieted the giggling with these gentle words: "Don't laugh; that's a beautiful desire." And for a few years after that, when we met in the school corridors, she would ask encouragingly, "Thomas, do you still want to become a priest?" I never forgot her kindness and made certain that this good woman received an invitation to my first Mass. We remained close friends until her death.

Why I'm Having So Much Fun

Why so much happiness and satisfaction in my priesthood? Two reason stand out. First of all, my pleasure at being productive. Sitting around doing nothing has never been for me the pinnacle of fun. I get more relaxation and joy from grabbing a hammer and nailing together some useful storage shelves, or better still, by giving an inspiring talk or two, or maybe even forty or so, as I've done each February for the past dozen years for Mother Teresa's Missionaries of Charity in Kolkata.

Sure, I know how to waste a bit of time, and I do so whenever I need to relax. Long vacations of doing nothing, however, have never been my style. For me, it's always more fun to be doing something helpful, and nothing could be more useful than working hard to continue the mission that God the Father gave his Son, who in turn gave it to the apostles as he ordained them with these empowering words: "As the Father has sent me, so I send you" (John 20:21).

And that brings me to the second reason for my happiness: the thrill of proclaiming the greatness and goodness of Jesus Christ. I've had the fun of doing that job for 55 years and in 109 different countries of the world—and with Dubai now on my calendar, that's about to become 110. How can anything be more satisfying and enjoyable than making the proclamation that Jesus Christ is not only our Brother and Friend, but also our Savior and King, our Lord and God? Just how much fun can anyone possibly have?

Meeting and serving God's loving children all around the world has meant me squeezing into cramped seats in planes that have flown somewhere between two and three million miles, perhaps even more. Even now, at the age of eighty-two, my flying days are still not over. A few dozen upcoming trips are already on my calendar, and when people sometimes ask me, "But Father, when are you going to retire?" I slip into my John Wayne impersonation and answer with a smile, "Actually, I'm planning to die with my boots on." These words for me don't mean "with my gun drawn," but rather, "with my mouth proclaiming the Good News of Christ's great mercy and love."

Once I met and spoke with a king and queen, and once I met a movie star. But as many as one hundred different times, I've met and spoken with two great saints—Pope John Paul II and Mother Teresa of Calcutta. In the Papal Audience Hall at Vatican City, I organized and preached at retreats for more than eleven thousand priests who had come from one hundred different countries.

I've had the thrill of carrying the Good News of Jesus Christ to the very ends of the earth. All I can say for the enjoyment of it all is "Thank you, dearest Jesus, my God and my King and the Source of all my joy!"

Fr. Tom Forrest, a Redemptorist priest, was ordained in New York in 1954. For twenty-three years, he worked among the poor of the Caribbean. For six years, beginning in 1978, he served as director of the International Office for Catholic Charismatic Renewal. He is currently international director of Evangelization 2000, a Catholic effort to promote Church renewal through prayer, proclamation of the Word, and evangelism. He resides in Washington, D.C.

Chapter 3

"I Will Not
Leave You Orphaned"

Fr. Daren J. Zehnle

I discerned a call to the priesthood through the many events of my life, some of which were very sad and painful. Yet it was in each one of these experiences that I most deeply felt my call to the priesthood as a call to share the love of Christ Jesus with a hurting world. These events seemed to come together, almost like a puzzle, and in them I was able to hear the Lord's will for my life.

To share my story, I need to start at the beginning. When I was about four years old, my mother developed a brain tumor, which confined her to a hospital bed in our home. I have a few very fond memories of Mom walking, but most of my memories are of her bedridden. After Mom's cancer developed, Dad stopped working as an electrician and stayed home to care for her, my brother, and me.

On February 20, 1986, my brother and I awoke as usual. We readied ourselves for school and only needed Dad to cook us breakfast before we got on the bus and were off to school. Oddly though, Dad was not up yet. Typically he was already in the kitchen, listening to the radio and fixing breakfast. My brother and I thought nothing about it, and when we were ready, I went to wake him up. Not finding him in his bedroom, I discovered him on the couch where he had fallen asleep the night before. I called his name and shook him, but Dad would not wake up. I woke Mom and she, too, tried to rouse him, but to no avail. Out of desperation, we called my Aunt Marie, who arrived shortly thereafter, but she could not wake Dad either. At long last we called the ambulance.

When the paramedics arrived, my brother and I were sent outside to wait with the neighbors who had come down to our house. If I remember the morning correctly, it was snowing lightly but was not chilly. The wait outside seemed like an eternity.

Finally, one of the paramedics stepped outside. He said not a word, but I can still see the look on his face as he sadly shook his head as though to say, "No, he did not make it; he is dead." The look on his face said it all. As soon as he stepped through the door, I knew, and I cried my heart out. I could do nothing but cry for the next two or three days. I was not quite eight years old.

I was, quite naturally, devastated. For a long time, I constantly asked God, "Why did you do this? How could you let this happen? What did I do to deserve this?" I simply could not understand.

I am not quite sure how I survived that experience, but I did. My brother and I moved in with Dad's sister, her husband, and their four children. Let me tell you, it was a houseful, especially when you count the dogs, cat, hamsters, and bird!

Mom was placed in a nursing home, and we visited her every week after Mass and other times throughout the week when we could. As time progressed, she grew steadily worse. On January 18, 1988, I was building yet another bigger and better Lego castle with my cousins when the telephone rang. My aunt then told me the purpose of the call: Mom had just died. I was not quite ten years old.

Why Me?

I was again devastated. Again the question of "Why?" emerged from deep within me. I could not grasp how God could take away the two most important people in my life, especially when I was so very young. I had done nothing wrong. I did not deserve this. Day after day I would ask God, "Why? Why me?" I also asked him countless times to return my parents to me. I remember wishing many times, "Star light, star bright, first star I see tonight. I wish I may, I wish I might, have this wish I wish tonight." Each time I thought those words, I asked for my mom and dad. I told no one of this wish. It never happened.

To this day I have not received an answer to my initial question, but as I continually questioned God, I slowly found myself praying, and in the midst of this prayer, I heard him say to me, "It is I. Do not be afraid" (John 6:20). "I will not leave you orphaned; I will come to you" (John 14:18, NRSV). "I am here. I love you."

And come to me he did: through the Scriptures, prayer, and the sacraments. I slowly came to know that "the Lamb who is in the center of the throne will shepherd them / and lead them to springs of life-giving water, / and God will wipe away every tear from their eyes" (Revelation 7:17). I began to feel the Lord's loving presence, and I began to ask him—subconsciously, but I asked him nonetheless—"Who are you, sir?" (Acts 9:5). As I listened to him in prayer, I came to know him, and I recognized him as "My Lord and my God" (John 20:28).

Growing up without my parents was very difficult indeed, and their deaths had a very profound impact on me. All of my personality traits and qualities can be traced back to their deaths in some fashion. Don't get me wrong: My aunt and uncle were both very good to me, and I could not have asked for better, but they could never take the place of my parents. This they realized, and never did they attempt to do so.

Experiencing God's Love

These many years later, I look back on these two events that shaped my very being with gratitude, not because of the loss of my parents, but rather because of how I grew and matured as a result of their deaths. After Dad died, but especially after Mom, I began to pray to God, asking him for answers, for support, and for love. As I spent more time in the presence of God, I felt his love in a very real way, and drew immense peace and comfort from that experience. In my great sadness and pain, I went to him, and there I experienced his love.

When I was seventeen, I went on my first Teens Encounter Christ (TEC) retreat. Here I was able, for the first time, to really let go of much of the hurt and pain that I had kept bottled up deep within me. It felt so good to be free of that pain after so many years, and with that release, the love of God seemed to flow through me. I could truly feel the healing presence of God in and around me.

God's presence to me was also manifested in the person of Fr. John Beveridge, the pastor at my parish. Fr. John helped me through these difficult experiences without even fully realizing that he had done so. He was always there for me from the moment I first arrived in the parish after Dad died. As I grew, so too did our friendship. He was always there with a listening spirit, a compassionate heart, helpful advice, a great joke, and an encouraging and loving spirit. Fr. John shared in all of my pains and in all of my joys; this I felt called to do for others.

My experiences of Fr. John's loving care and concern for me, together with my experiences of God's deep love for me, began to foster within me a desire to serve the Lord. This desire developed through grade school and especially into high school as I became more involved with the parish and with the TEC community.

Then in high school, I began to feel God stirring within my heart, calling me to into his service as a priest. I heard his voice in "a tiny whispering sound" in the stillness of my heart (1 Kings 19:12). I came to realize that his love, which I had experienced and had come to rely upon, required me to give it to others; I could not keep it to myself. I heard him calling: "Whom shall I send? Who will go for us?" (Isaiah 6:8). As he called to the apostles, so he called to me: "Come after me, and I will make you fishers of men" (Matthew 4:19). But unlike the apostles, I did not immediately leave everything to follow him. I said, "I am too young" (Jeremiah 1:6), and he responded: "Follow me" (Mark 2:14).

Even so, I thought myself unworthy of so generous a calling—indeed, I am unworthy of it. There were others in my parish more fit for his service, I thought. There were others more popular, more intelligent, more talented, more loving than I, and so I at first declined his invitation, choosing instead to teach history. I could not see why the Lord wanted me, wounded as I was. I did not yet realize that, as Thornton Wilder wrote, "In Love's service, only wounded soldiers can serve."

After my first TEC weekend, I could not decide exactly what I wanted to do with my life, whether I wanted to teach history or become a priest. I told no one about what the Lord was saying to me, which made even more remarkable what soon happened after: At this point of indecision, many parishioners approached me before, during, and after Mass and told me, "You should think about the priesthood; you'd make a good priest." I was stunned.

Within a matter of weeks, it was not simply a handful of my fellow parishioners saying this to me, but dozens, and the number grew with each passing week. They never pushed or shoved; they simply commented. But even with such affirmations, I still was unsure. I knew that I was not worthy of so great a calling, but who of us is?

A Flashing Light

At one point I decided that I wanted to teach history and yet, as is often the case with God, the desire for the priesthood never left me. It was like a light flashing in the back of my mind, blinking in an irritating way, as if to say, "Hey, look at me!" And so I did. I looked closer at and prayed about the priesthood, and came to the conclusion that this is God's call for me: to be a priest. The priesthood simply seemed as though it would fit my personality and my desires, and I somehow knew that only as a priest would I ever find joy, contentment, fulfillment, and peace.

After I made this decision, the thought of teaching history no longer appealed to me. (Now, as a priest, I teach Church history in our parish high school.) Meanwhile, signs of God's call became more and more apparent. I grew more in love with helping at the parish and in the TEC community, and this continued through my college years as I devoted most of my time to campus ministry and the RCIA program. All through college, the desire to serve God as a priest only grew.

After receiving a bachelor's degree in history, I went to study and be formed for the priesthood at the University of St. Mary of the Lake/Mundelein Seminary. I was ordained to the priesthood of Jesus Christ on May 28, 2005, for service in the Diocese of Springfield in Illinois.

If, after reading this, you find yourself asking, "What does the Lord want of me?" ask yourself three simple and basic questions:

Where do I find joy?
Where do I find peace?
Where do I find fulfillment?

Where these three answers coincide, there I am certain is God's will.

And if you find yourself asking, "Lord, why me?" ask yourself instead, "Why *not* me?"

Fr. Zehnle is pastor of Sacred Heart Parish in Virden, Illinois, and of St. Patrick Parish in Girard, Illinois. This story is adapted from one appearing on his blog, "Servant and Steward," at www.servantandsteward.org.

Chapter 4

Making Prayer
the Center of My Life

Fr. James Hudgins

The turning point in my priesthood was the day I decided to place prayer at the center of my life. You may assume that prayer is at the center of the life of every priest, or that priests do not have to struggle to find time to pray. While this is partially true, since we offer Mass each day and have promised to pray the Liturgy of the Hours, the fact is that many priests claim that they are "too busy" to spend much time in prayer. I once said the same thing. My life changed when I stopped telling myself that, and now my only regret is that I did not make that change even sooner.

When I was ordained in May 1998, my prayer life consisted of the Rosary, the Mass, and the Liturgy of the Hours. I had always been faithful in my prayers, and I considered myself to have a solid prayer life.

I knew that every priest was *alter Christus*, "another Christ," and that each priest was only as effective in his ministry as he was like his divine Master. In all my parish activities—teaching in the grade school, visiting the sick, preparing people to receive the sacraments, counseling, and advising—I knew that my own holiness was inadequate. I needed the holiness of the saints, the holiness of Christ himself, or I would never reach the hearts of my people. I certainly did not have that holiness, and what was worse, I was no better with each passing day.

Spiritually speaking, I was stagnant and frustrated. In my priesthood I sensed something was missing. Despite the dutiful, observant, and faithful execution of my tasks, despite my faithful completion of the prayers I had promised to pray, such as the Mass and the Liturgy of the Hours, I knew something was missing. I was searching for a deeper, more personal union with Christ, but I was unable to find it.

I had the good fortune to receive spiritual direction from Fr. Thomas Dubay, a regular on EWTN and a world-renowned author of nearly thirty books on prayer and the spiritual life. Fr. Dubay helped me to see that prayer is more than the execution of a task, but rather the union of Christ with the soul—a deeply personal, intimate matter that needs a generous offering of time each day.

Sacrificing Time to Spend with God

When Fr. Dubay told me that I must dedicate much more time to prayer than I ever had before, I replied (as most people do), "I do not have time for more prayer. I am too busy." He told me I was fooling myself. Absolutely everyone can claim that they are "too busy." We must be disciplined about how we use our time, and we must sacrifice time, in faith, to spend it in prayer.

I protested, "No, it is impossible. There is no more time." He firmly contradicted me and directed me to add one half hour of silent prayer to my day—every day. He promised that if I did, it would produce great changes in my life and in my priesthood, and that if I did not, I would never emerge from the state of spiritual stagnation and frustration that I was living.

I resolved to give it a try. I knew the only "extra" time to pray was in the early morning. In all my life, I had never been a morning person. Once, in fact, I had overslept and missed my own scheduled Mass—at 9:00 a.m.! But with so many events rushing upon me unpredictably each day, I knew I had no choice: If I wanted to pray, I simply had to wake up early and do it.

Much to my surprise, I discovered that Fr. Dubay was exactly right. I began to experience a transformation in every aspect of my priesthood and in my own life as a Christian. I had more energy. I had more patience. Sins and temptations began to weaken and diminish: idle chatter, wasting time, petty bitterness and complaints, unforgiveness, fear of the opinions of others—countless personal faults began to melt away like a late winter snow. Most surprising of all was the effect it had on all my other prayers. The Mass, the Rosary, the Liturgy of the Hours—these all became deeper, more personal, and more meaningful than they had ever been before.

Before long I had no trouble "finding" time to pray. A mysterious, ever-increasing presence of Christ in my soul made it easy to "find" time. My prayer time was *his* time, and whereas before I had seen prayer as a duty to be completed, I now began to see it as a privileged time with Christ, which made me a better priest, all day long, for everyone else I met.

I believe prayer is the key to transforming every Christian life, but that the commitment to spend time each day in prayer is not easy to make. I offer my story to help encourage anyone to make that commitment—for your own good and the good of others.

I am the chaplain of a large Catholic high school outside Washington, D.C., ministering each day to young people who are very good-hearted but also very misdirected by the society they live in. I wake up each morning and spend an hour and a half before the Blessed Sacrament, praying for myself and all the students in the school. My prayer life allows Christ to work though me for their benefit. On my own I can do nothing, but with Christ working through me, I can bring his presence to them. Prayer makes this possible.

The same holds true for any Christian: mothers and fathers who want to be the best possible parents for their children; family members who need to forgive one another and put away old bitterness; all who know that their own best efforts are not enough and who yearn for "something more."

Nothing has changed my life and my priesthood more than the decision to dedicate time to prayer, and for anyone who wants to transform his or her own life in Christ, there is nothing I can recommend more highly.

Fr. James Hudgins was born in St. Louis, Missouri, and lived in several different states before being ordained in 1998 for the Diocese of Arlington, Virginia. He has served at several parishes in the diocese and is currently a high school chaplain at Bishop O'Connell High School in Arlington.

Chapter 5

Certainty, Commitment, and Joy

Fr. Alfredo Hernández

Why am I a priest? I once read a book with that question as the title, and I was moved by the responses of my brother priests. It led me to reflect on that question myself. After seventeen years as a priest, I definitely have some answers, some of which have been constant over these years and some of which have changed with time.

When people ask me why I became a priest, often they have no clue what the life of a priest is like. They consider it to be a life only of denials—of not having one's own family or home or the opportunity to do what any man ought to be able to do. Others imagine the life of a priest as something boring—hence the question, "So, Father, what do you do after morning Mass?" Or worse, "What do you do from Monday to Friday?" Even those who understand the hard work that the priesthood entails (or certainly should entail if lived well) too frequently imagine it as something sad and depressing, not a life that can bring joy and happiness to the priest himself.

What God Wants for Me

The first reason I would give for why I am a priest is that I am sure this is what God wants for me. When I was twenty-three years old, I was working as a college administrator in the Northeast. I was considering the priesthood, but at the same time, I was thinking about marriage and a family. A woman I was dating, who was a very good Catholic, finally asked me point-blank, "How are you going to make up your mind? Are you waiting for a bolt of lightning to hit you?"

In a way that question *was* the bolt of lightning, because the next day I picked up the rosary and prayed with an open heart for the first time in a long time. The mystery of the annunciation hit me right between the eyes. From that moment I have never doubted that God was asking me for a yes like Mary's, a total yes to his will. Since that night I have been sure that the yes to which he was calling me was—and still is—the priesthood.

When I work with couples preparing for marriage or with spouses experiencing some relationship difficulty, I will often ask them to tell me how they fell in love. The memory of that first moment, in which a man and a woman first realize that it is God's plan for them to share their lives, is something very important for them to keep close to their hearts. In difficult moments it will give them hope that nothing they are facing can undermine the love that God has given them. In the same way, it is important for me (and I daresay for every priest) to recall the moment in which I "fell in love" with the priesthood, so that I can live it well, with its joys and sorrows.

Free to Love

But I am a priest not only because of the certainty that I felt at the age of twenty-three. I am also a priest because of the commitments I made when I was ordained a deacon in 1991 and a priest in 1992. I am a priest because I trust that God will give me the help I need to fulfill these commitments. There is a certain allergy to commitment today. Many people wonder how it is possible to keep a promise forever, especially since we are as changeable as we are. Experience has shown me, however, that we can only hope to be truly happy if we are able to keep firm the commitments we make—to marriage, to religious life, to the priesthood, or to whatever vocation God calls us.

A life of commitment is not a burden to carry but rather the only way we can be truly free to love as God wants us to love. This is as true for the married person as for the priest. One thing that has come to me only recently is how important it is to thank God for the call to the priesthood. I often tell couples at their wedding to thank God for the gift of their spouse each morning and each night. It has helped me to apply this advice to myself. I thank God each day for the gift he has given me, of knowing that it is precisely as a priest that he wants me to love him and to love his people. Fulfilling the commitments I made when I was ordained is not a terrible burden but a cause of joy.

And it *is* a joy to live my priesthood. I do not pretend that it is easy, but over the last seventeen years, the Lord has always found ways to show me that he is with me in the work that he has commended to me and to which I have committed myself—and this is what gives me joy. He blesses me through the supportive words of parishioners, through deep moments of prayer, and through particularly beautiful liturgies. He blesses me through unexpected conversions, or through the person who says to me, "Bless me, Father, it has been thirty years since my last confession." Certainly, every time I celebrate the Mass, it is a confirmation that God has given me an unsurpassable gift.

So the priesthood is not sad, depressing, or boring. Despite what the world tells us, any life lived faithfully in response to God's call is a way to happiness. I can say that I am a priest filled with joy because God continues to work in me, today and every day.

Fr. Alfredo I. Hernández, VF, was raised in Palm Beach, Florida, and earned undergraduate and graduate degrees at the University of Florida before entering St. Vincent de Paul Regional Seminary in Boynton Beach. He was ordained a priest in 1992 and received a Licentiate of Sacred Theology from the Gregorian University in Rome. He is currently pastor of his home parish, St. Juliana, West Palm Beach. He is also dean of the Central Deanery of the Diocese of Palm Beach and an adjunct faculty member at St. Vincent de Paul Regional Seminary.

Chapter 6

The Lessons I Learned from My Hispanic Parishioners

Msgr. Scott Friend

After my ordination I was assigned to work with the growing number of Hispanic immigrants in my diocese. Most of them were from Mexico, but just about every Latin country was represented among them. They have taught me many lessons and have helped me depend on God for everything. They have especially taught me to be the priest that God has called me to be. Here are three of those lessons.

A Providential God

In the first part of my priestly life, I was assigned to develop Hispanic ministry in the diocese. I would drive three thousand miles around the diocese every month, knocking on doors looking for immigrants, and I would celebrate Masses in different parishes. At this time I was still very impressed with my own beauty and abilities, so I would ask God for help if I really needed it, but mostly I ran off my own energy.

So it is not surprising that I got discouraged after a short while. I would drive several hours for a Mass, and only ten or twenty people would show up. I was frustrated and not sure what to do. I was also very cynical about things, although I tried not to show it.

Around the end of October in my third year of the priesthood, I went to St. Luke's Parish for the monthly Mass and a meeting that followed with the leaders of the parish. They told me, "Padre, we are making plans for the Mass for Our Lady of Guadalupe in December. We are going to have a big fiesta to feed everyone who will come. We have enough beans and rice, but we don't have enough meat. Could you find us a deer?" I thought to myself, "This is it! All the time I spent in school, all the training that I've had, and these people want me to find a deer as if they grow on trees." So I said, "*Si Dios quiere*," which means "God willing." However, I really meant it sarcastically!

The following Tuesday, I got a call from a man I'd never met before who wanted to talk about Hispanic ministry. I invited him to come the next morning for Mass. After Mass I greeted everyone, and this man stayed back until everyone had left. I am used to the usual formalities when I meet someone for the first time, but this guy came up with trembling hands and said to me, "Father, do you have a sharp knife and some plastic bags?" Now, I have watched enough cable movies to know that you don't give your own knife to someone, so I asked him what was going on. His answer made my hair stand on end.

"On the way over this morning, I hit a deer, and it is in the back of my car! I need to drain the blood from the deer so that the meat doesn't spoil." I was speechless. I went into the rectory, got the knife and the bags, and went with him to his car.

Sure enough, there was a dead deer in the back of this car with its tongue sticking out. I began to question the man, because my mind did not want to believe what was happening. I asked him to tell me how this happened. He said that it was really strange. It was a beautiful morning, the sun was shining, and he was enjoying the drive. He noticed up ahead the deer eating grass on the side of the road. He said that when he got close to the deer, it lifted its head, looked him right in the eye, and just walked in front of his car and gave up its life. Those were his exact words!

While it is not unusual to hit a deer in Arkansas, it is rare when it occurs in the daytime. Another thing the man did not understand: There was no visible damage to the car, not even a scratch—only some fur on the bumper. The man said he was still trembling from the experience.

I didn't want to let on that it was my fault that all of this had happened! But I finally gave in and said to him, "I am supposed to ask you for some of this deer meat." He did not say anything; he just cut off the back hindquarter and gave it to me. I carried it back to the rectory, and I said to God, "You don't have to be so dramatic!" I could hear God rolling on the floor, dying from laughter.

The following week I went to the parish and handed the deer meat to Ana, one of the leaders, and said rather enthusiastically, "Here's your deer meat." She just took it like she was expecting that it was coming, so I said, "Wait a minute—this was a miracle!" I will never forget the look on her face. She said to me, "You're a priest, and you don't know that God is providential!" I got the lesson! I have come to rely on God and to ask with faith, knowing that the Lord will listen.

The Gift of Priesthood

I was invited to a village in the state of Guanajuato in Mexico, the hometown of many of my parishioners. After a twenty-four hour drive, we finally arrived, and I was asked to celebrate Mass in a neighboring town the next day. Lots of people came to that Mass, and afterward they all gathered around me. They were taking my hands and kissing them, which is a custom that is still practiced in rural areas in Mexico. It is a way of acknowledging that a priest's hands are consecrated. They were also reaching out and touching me as if I were something sacred. I must admit that it made me feel very strange.

It was just about this time that I felt that I had left my body in some way and was looking down at myself, and I felt Jesus present next to me. I understood him to say, "They think you are holy!" I told the Lord, "Imagine that!" He said to me, "These people are here to remind you that you are my priest now. It is my priesthood you carry, and it is my priesthood they are reverencing, and it is I who chose you to be a priest for them."

The next thing I knew, I was back with everyone. A religious sister came up to me, accompanied by a woman whose son had fallen sick and was too weak to get out of bed. She asked me to come and pray over him. Off we went—the mother, the sister, myself, and everyone else! I have to admit, I was afraid. I prayed to the Lord, "Hey, are you still here? These people are expecting a miracle." The house was right across the street from the chapel, a small adobe home with dirt floors and just two rooms. I went to the young man, who was just a teenager, and we talked for a while. I laid my hands that had been kissed so many times that evening on his forehead and I prayed, believing now in the priesthood that I carried.

Before I left, I was asked to return the following Sunday to say Mass again. When I arrived, I was startled by the sound of fireworks. "What are they celebrating?" I asked. I discovered that the fireworks were for me! Then I spotted the boy whom I had prayed over, standing there, perfectly healthy. I was astounded!

We celebrated Mass, and I was deeply moved, because during the offertory, the people all brought up different types of food, such as fruit and cheese. I really had to hold back tears because I thought to myself, "Here these poor people are bringing something for those who are even poorer." After Mass I asked the sacristan if it was their custom to bring food for the poor every Sunday. He looked at me strangely and said, "That food is not for the poor. That food is for you!"

It turns out that I was the poor person that day. What I took away from that place was a new understanding that I had been given the Lord's priesthood, and that it was real and powerful. I realized that being a priest means that you are a priest all the time, wherever you go, and I was now aware of the presence of Christ with me. Wherever I went from then on, I knew that the Lord's priesthood would be accessible to people through me, and that his presence could even bring healing.

Becoming a Sacrifice

About seven years ago, I began to have problems that eventually led to a series of medical tests, including a lumbar puncture. I knew the outcome couldn't be good, and when I went to the neurologist's office for the report, he told me, "You have multiple sclerosis." It was devastating. I had a priest friend with the disease, and he was fairly disabled with it.

It took me a while to accept the diagnosis. The doctors told me that they don't know what causes MS, that there is no cure for it, and that there would be no way to tell how it would affect me. That is why they affectionately call it a very "personal" disease— it affects each person differently. All I knew was that I could lose the ability to walk, talk, or see. My memory would probably be affected. MS takes away all of your psychological security, which is a false sense of security, but nonetheless, I was afraid.

I came to prayer one day feeling particularly sorry for myself. I had just one big question: WHY? The Lord was waiting for me, and he spoke to me in prayer. This happened just about the time when the pedophilia crisis was surfacing. The Lord said to me, "Look, we are good friends, and friends ask favors of each other, so I want to ask you a favor. Carry this disease for me. Show people what it means to be my priest. So many people are hurt by what is happening. Help them by carrying this disease as a gift." It was an offer I couldn't refuse, and it changed the way I saw things. I asked the Lord for the grace to be able to suffer with joy whatever would happen to me. The many Hispanics that I had served had taught me about living, and even suffering, with joy!

I really began to see what it means to offer sacrifice as a priest. Now I would be offering my own life. Every Thursday I would take a shot of interferon. The doctors stated that there might be side effects, but that they would go away after a few months on the drug. They never went away for me. Every Thursday I knew that a few hours after I had the shot, I would experience symptoms that imitated the flu. I decided to not let the suffering go to waste, so I began to offer it for different things. One of those was for the conversion of all the parishioners in my parish, but occasions would arise that I would specifically choose to suffer for.

One day the parish secretary told me that a man from her village, Saul, had suffered a stroke. The family requested that I go to the hospital to anoint him. When I got to the hospital, things didn't look good. The doctor told me that there was no chance for Saul. He had so much bleeding in his brain that he would probably be in a coma for the rest of his life. If he did by chance come out of the coma, he would probably remain in a vegetative state.

I went to his wife, Susanna, and explained what the doctor had told me. I related to her that the doctor not only recommended that no surgery be performed, but that the best thing to do was to turn off the respirator and let nature take its course. Susanna looked at me and said that her children needed their father and that she needed her husband. She wanted to do everything possible with the hope that he be healed. She asked me to anoint him.

We all gathered around Saul in his room. I talked to Saul, not just with words, but also with all my heart. I told him that he was going to receive the anointing of the sick, but that he also had to fight to get well. We all prayed, and I anointed Saul. It just happened to be a Wednesday, and so I told Saul that I was going to suffer for him the next day and offer that to God for him to get better. I said that to him knowing, as St. John of the Cross says, that "prayer is the only power to which God surrenders."

I got my shot on Thursday morning and offered the side effects for Saul's healing. On Saturday I returned to my parish after some meetings at the diocese and found it strange that I had heard nothing about Saul. So after evening Mass, I went to the hospital to Saul's room in the intensive care unit. Much to my surprise, I was told that he had been moved to a regular room.

I went to his room and there he was, very awake and talking to his family! He was not even on the respirator, and he actually remembered everything I had said to him while he was in a coma! His wife told me that beginning on Thursday morning, his body began to absorb the blood in his brain, and that by Thursday evening, Saul began to wake up. Saul did suffer some paralysis on his left side, but he was eventually able to walk.

This past spring Saul's daughter made her confirmation, and she asked me to be her sponsor. After the Mass we all went to dinner, and all I could feel was gratitude for being able to have dinner with Saul and his family six years after he was left for dead. I would never have thought when I was first diagnosed with MS that I would someday be grateful for the disease that brought healing to this family. I was also grateful to the Lord for asking me to do him a favor and humbled that he would allow me to live his priesthood so intimately.

I am indebted to all the people who I have had the pleasure of serving in the great Diocese of Little Rock. They pray for us priests, and they put up with us! I know that our diocese is the Lord's favorite part of his vineyard, and I am thankful that he has called me to be a priest here. But I am especially grateful to the Hispanics in my diocese and those I have come to know through them in Mexico and other places in Latin America. They have helped me learn how to live for something greater than myself: a priest of Our Lord Jesus!

Msgr. Scott Friend was born in Little Rock, Arkansas, in 1961. He attended St. Meinrad Seminary and was ordained a priest on June 20, 1987. Currently, he is vicar general and vocation director of the Diocese of Little Rock. He is especially grateful to work with the seminarians of the Diocese of Little Rock and sees great hope for the Church in the young men being called to the priesthood in his diocese.

Chapter 7

Becoming a Priest Every Day

Fr. Cedric Pisegna, CP

I remember seeing a billboard once that showed a graphic portrayal of Jesus suffering on the cross. Underneath was the caption "Be a priest like me." It was a startling message for vocations. There's no doubt that the priesthood requires sacrifice. You must be a man for others. It demands self-denial, discipline, and giving of self. On the day of my ordination, June 29, 1991, my character was indelibly etched by Jesus and changed.

However, the actual realization of who I am as a priest is gradual and lifelong. I like to say, "I was ordained a priest in 1991, but I am *becoming* a priest every day." I am growing in patience, generosity, and love for others. I am learning to trust in God. Two aspects of my priesthood have especially helped me to become the priest that I am. One is hearing confessions, and the other is sharing my faith with young people. Both have brought me great joy.

Touched by Christ in the Confessional

I have to admit that when I was first ordained, I thought it might be burdensome or strange to hear confessions. Yet through these years, I've been surprised at just how powerful the Sacrament of Reconciliation really is. I've heard thousands of confessions, and I never cease to be amazed at how Christ touches us in this sacrament.

Many people are nervous when they come to celebrate this sacrament. Once a woman came in, and instead of praying, "Bless me, Father, for I have sinned," she said, "Bless us, O Lord, and these thy gifts." I half expected her to break out some food so we could celebrate. Actually, we laughed about her nervous start, and it became a moment of relaxation for her.

The trust people give priests is inspiring. There are no masks in the confessional—people are extremely honest and vulnerable. I see them at their best as well as at their worst. They share their hidden secrets and tell me things they haven't even shared with their spouses. I try to provide a nonjudgmental, safe place where people can open up fully.

The Twelve-Step Program has a saying: "You are only as sick as your secrets." When people share their innermost secrets and sins with me, I know they are letting the light of God in and moving forward. A process toward freedom begins. Healing occurs. Issues are confronted. Forgiveness and mercy are received. The founder of the Passionists order, St. Paul of the Cross, said he preached in order to get people to come to confession. He knew the power of what could happen one-on-one in that sacrament.

I am surprised not only in what happens in the penitent but also in me. When I hear you share honestly and with complete vulnerability, I find that my heart becomes very soft. As I look into your eyes and listen to your struggles, in some ways you reflect my life, as if I am looking into a mirror. Your wrestling to forgive others, overcome your compulsions, and be sincerely devoted to God confronts me with my own struggles and helps me resolve to try harder and address the same issues in my life. Your honesty is a witness to me. We are not islands unto ourselves but are all part of the same continent. We share a common humanity, and my communion with you is profound as you share.

Reaching Out to Young People

Before I was ordained, I was a youth minister, so I have a special place in my heart for young people. I believe that one of our primary roles as priests is to reach out to our young. As a priest, I have had many opportunities to speak with our youth in large gatherings as well as one-on-one. They are so gifted and energetic. I see such potential and such hunger. I so want them to become all they can be and to discover God's plan for their lives.

I remember the largest Mass I ever attended, the Mass that concluded World Youth Day in Denver in August 1993. We celebrated outdoors at Cherry Creek State Park. Pope John Paul II presided, and I was one of three thousand priests concelebrating. There were people as far as the eye could see. Some estimated the crowd at half to three quarters of a million people. Most of those present were teenagers.

I encountered one young man when I was preaching the "call to the mission" at the well-to-do St. Stephen's Church in Orlando, Florida. I had just preached my homily about having a personal relationship with Jesus. After Mass a good-looking sixteen-year-old boy with blonde hair approached me. He was adorned with a gold chain around his neck, and he had an urgency about his appeal. He reminded me of the rich young man in the gospels.

"Father," he said, "look around at this building. Beautiful, isn't it?" I looked around at the huge sanctuary and glistening marble floors. "Yes, this is one of the finest churches I've ever been in," I agreed. He continued: "My parents have poured lots of money into the building fund to get this place built. Week after week they make me come to church. I have to admit I don't know the God we worship. I don't know the God for whom this building has been built. But when I heard you talking about knowing God in a personal way, something in me stirred. Can you help me?" "Yes," I said. "Let that hunger you feel in your heart guide you, and you will come to know God. God is real and is calling you to know him in an intimate way."

I see priesthood as an opportunity. It stretches my limits. I am tapping into inner resources and potential I never knew I had. I continue to launch out into the deep "for a catch." When I was ordained, I resolved that I wouldn't just "get by" or "drift." I want to live with *passion* and impact as many people as I can in as deep a way as possible for Jesus. For me, priesthood is packed with meaning, purpose, and significance. Whether I am preaching, writing, producing, counseling, hearing confessions, or meeting with youth, I am very fulfilled.

I heard a saying years ago that I have adopted as the foundation of my ministry: "Who you are is God's gift to you. Who you *become* is your gift to God." Priesthood is all about becoming your best and presenting your life to God as a gift. It involves striving to achieve your potential and inviting others to live with passion. Because of this priestly call, I have gone where I never thought I would go, met people who I never would have met, and am becoming someone I never dreamed I could be. That graphic billboard stays in my mind: "Be a priest like me."

Fr. Cedric Pisegna, CP, is a Passionist priest who preaches parish missions across the United States. He has authored thirteen books, including God's Not Boring! *for young people.* He also produces a television program Live with Passion!, *which airs in numerous cities.* His Web site site is *www.frcedric.org.*

Chapter 8

Lord, Make Me an Instrument of Your Peace

Fr. John Dear, SJ

I entered the Jesuits in 1982 and was ordained in 1993. At the time I could never have imagined how this path would take me in so many directions. But of all my many experiences, the days after September 11, 2001, most embody to me what it means to be a priest.

As I wrote in my autobiography, *A Persistent Peace*, I was living in New York City at the time and had just stepped down as director of the Fellowship of Reconciliation. That Thursday morning, after the Twin Towers had fallen, I walked down to the hastily assembled Family Assistance Center, set up in the old armory on Lexington Avenue, to volunteer.

Thousands of worried, crying relatives lined the street. They waited for hours to fill out a missing-person report and glean what information they could. Inside the place was packed with police officers, Red Cross officials, and desperate New Yorkers. A Red Cross official asked me to stand in the corner. "After everyone has filled out their paperwork, we'll send them to you for spiritual counseling," she said. "All you have to do is listen and be a compassionate presence." For the next three months, I tried to be that compassionate presence of peace. During my tenure, I met one-on-one with some fifteen hundred grieving relatives.

After that first day, I was asked to serve as a local coordinator for the Red Cross chaplains at the Family Assistance Center. I agreed. More than 550 chaplains from every religion ministered under my supervision. I worked out difficulties in scheduling and problems of security. I gave orientations to each new chaplain and debriefed each one at the end of every shift, and I taught others to do the same. None of the chaplains were to leave the center until we had gathered together and prayed and shared how each was bearing up. And no one was dismissed before telling the group what he or she planned to do that night for relaxation and rest. I took on no chaplains who refused to participate in those daily sessions. It was a lesson for all, including me, in the fine art of pastoral care and compassionate listening. You had to take care of yourself if you were going to be of service to others.

On September 14, the day after I had assumed my role as coordinator, I ventured to Ground Zero, where my eyes met destruction on a scale beyond imagining. With every block closer, the senses were struck harder. Blocks had been obliterated, sixteen acres all told, with many buildings hit by debris from the two towers. Everything was covered in white ash. At the World Trade Center plaza rose "the Pile," a mound of steel and rubble looming seven stories high. Smoke billowed forth, flames here and there. The stench was overpowering.

Hundreds of rescue workers poked about, tugging on fragments of girders and masses of stone, coming periodically upon a body. In my clerical attire and yellow hard hat, with a security pass slung around my neck, I was an incongruous sight. I marched right up to the edge of the site and stood there, overcome with astonishment, nausea, and grief.

Within seconds a fireman came scrambling down the Pile, ran up to me, and said, "Father, quick, give me your blessing. I'm digging for my best friend." I uttered a prayer and off he dashed, back up the Pile like a squirrel up a tree.

"Teach Me How to Pray"

For the rest of the day, workers accosted me—desperate to talk, overwhelmed by grief, exhausted, and running on adrenaline. One begged, "Father, please, teach me how to pray. We found the body of my friend yesterday, and I just don't know what to do." No one had ever before asked me how to pray. Never had I been pressed for such large answers in such short order, much less before such a sight. "God loves you very much," I told him, "so just turn to God, ask for help and guidance, and keep on doing that for the rest of your life."

For hours scores of people approached me, grief stricken and tired. I remember one man in particular, Emilio, a friendly police officer. It was his task to sort torsos and limbs, and he woke up each night after ghastly dreams, screaming at the top of his lungs. "What should I do, Father?" he asked me.

Back in the Family Assistance Center, I met countless poor souls. Mary, a security guard employed on the seventieth floor of the North Tower, clambered down flights of stairs and broke for daylight just before the collapse—all her co-workers presumably died, and her poor self trembling still. When I met Neil, a Long Island Catholic, he was clutching a bag of hairs snatched from a comb—a DNA specimen from his missing brother-in-law. In his case the body had been found, one of the few intact. Neil hunched over hours of paperwork; then, in tears, he placed the dreaded call to the family. I got him through as best I could and sent him on his way with a blessing and a prayer.

Then there was the family of twelve who flew in from Europe in search of a missing son. I bestowed a blessing and each in turn offered me a hug and a kiss. And the retired New Jersey couple searching for their son: I sat by as their mouths were swabbed for DNA. And the crying and quaking young man who flew in from Italy all by himself in hopes of finding his mother; and the businessman who had lost fifty colleagues. At Ground Zero I met the dozen firefighters just arrived from Mexico—a gift from the Mexican government—diminutive and scrappy, awaiting their chance to attack the Pile. "Please lead us in prayer, Padre," they said. We joined hands, I murmured my prayer, and they burst into tears. Then off they went, up the Pile. So many people, a blur in my battered memory, all of them crying out.

Throughout those days, I felt like John comforting Mary at the foot of the cross. That became an image of my priestly vocation.

The Ministry of Reconciliation

Thousands died at the World Trade Center towers, one hundred twenty-five at the Pentagon, and sixty-four more in the plane crash near Pittsburgh. We mourned them all. But in the weeks after September 11th, as the U.S. prepared to bomb Afghanistan and Iraq, my friends and I sought a way to carry on Jesus' peacemaking, pastoral work. We knew that retaliation was not the way of Jesus; that someone needed to stand up and say so; that we had to try to stop the impending wars.

And so during the day, I counseled and consoled grieving relatives of the 9/11 attacks; at night and on weekends, I organized and spoke at antiwar rallies across the nation. For me, it was all one work—the ministry of reconciliation that St. Paul writes about (2 Corinthians 5:18-19)—the priestly ministry of all believers: the task of healing, disarming, and inviting one another to embark anew on the path of gospel nonviolence in the footsteps of the peacemaking Jesus.

With various church friends, we organized prayer vigils, pro-peace rallies, and antiwar demonstrations from Times Square to Union Square, speaking out clearly against the U.S. bombing campaigns in Afghanistan and Iraq. And I did so as a priest. I was trying to model and teach the gospel message: Love your neighbors *and* love your enemies. I wanted to offer compassion both at home and abroad. I wanted to practice the unusual, universal love that Jesus teaches in the Sermon on the Mount.

That October I spoke to one thousand people at an antiwar rally in Greenwich Village. "Violence doesn't work," I said. "Violence in response to violence only leads to further violence. War cannot stop terrorism because war is terrorism. War never brings peace. Jesus calls us instead to love our enemies. We should stop U.S. militarism in the Middle East, dismantle our nuclear weapons, and reach out to those in need around the world to cut the roots of terrorism. We should build schools in Afghanistan, send food and medicine to Iraq, and teach the nonviolence of Jesus around the world. If we did, no one would want to hurt us again. Our nonviolent love would save us and lead us all to a new world without war or violence."

The crowd cheered that day, but the message of peace was usually not well received. But being a priest, as a chancellor once told me, is not a popularity contest. It means telling people that God loves them, that God is a God of love and peace, and that we are called to be people of peace. It means teaching everyone to be nonviolent to themselves, nonviolent to their spouses and children, nonviolent to other church people, and nonviolent to the world; to join the global grassroots movements of nonviolence that are disarming and healing the world.

Priestly peacemaking leads others to turn in prayer to the God of peace, to practice contemplative nonviolence, to allow God to disarm our hearts of the roots of war within us so that we might welcome the risen Jesus' gift of peace and pursue the end of war.

That's the whole point of being a priest—not to be powerful, not to be in control, not to dominate others or get attention or live in luxury or raise money or administer structures or claim any special privileges. The point is to serve Jesus—to be with him, lead others to him, discover him around us, share him in the Eucharist, and advocate his reign of nonviolence, that new world without war, poverty, nuclear weapons, or global warming.

Priests should try to embody and teach St. Francis' prayer: "Lord, make me an instrument of your peace." That was my experience in those difficult days after September 11th, and it remains my journey today—that where there is hatred, I might sow love; where there is despair and darkness, I might sow hope and light; where there is war, I might sow peace. I can honestly say that my prayer is being answered. Each step on the journey is a blessing of Christ's peace.

Fr. John Dear is a Jesuit priest, writer, lecturer, and peace activist. He is the author of twenty-five books, including Transfiguration, Living Peace, The Questions of Jesus, *and* The God of Peace. *He writes a weekly column for the* National Catholic Reporter *at www.ncroline.org. He was recently nominated for the Nobel Peace Prize by Archbishop Desmond Tutu. For further information, see www.johndear.org. This article was adapted from* A Persistent Peace: One Man's Struggle for a Nonviolent World.

Chapter 9

"Priest" and "Victim" with Christ

Fr. Andrew Apostoli, CFR

When I was only six years old, I became an altar boy. Learning the Latin responses at that time was certainly a challenge. One day as I was serving at the altar, a feeling came over me and I thought, "I want to do what the priest is doing!" At the time, I certainly didn't understand what the Mass was really all about, but something—we might call it the "mystery" of the priestly call—came over me and left an impression that I can still remember today. And it has been the Mass, and the reality it celebrates, that best reflects what the priesthood means to me.

In grade school the thought of becoming a priest slipped to the back of my mind. But in the seventh and eighth grade, it returned. Then a priest came to preach a mission at my parish. We were brought over to the church to hear him speak. He gave me a piece of advice that was to hasten me on my journey: "If you are thinking about becoming a priest, go and speak with one of the priests in your parish."

I took his advice and spoke to a newly ordained Capuchin Franciscan priest. He took me to visit a Capuchin seminary, where the student brothers were studying philosophy and theology. I spent the day with them. They seemed so happy. All I could think was "I want the happiness they have."

At the age of fourteen, I went off to a high school seminary, where I completed my high school studies. I then entered the Capuchin novitiate, and after my profession of temporary vows, I did my college studies, focusing on philosophy. After my final vows, I began four years of theology studies Toward the end of my last year, on March 16, 1967, I was ordained a priest by Bishop Fulton J. Sheen, who was then bishop of the Diocese of Rochester, New York.

It was a long journey through the seminary. Sometimes it appeared that I might never reach the goal of priesthood. But once I was ordained, time has just flown by, and I have come to appreciate the beautiful gift God gave me when Bishop Sheen placed his hands on my head and conferred the power of the priesthood by bestowing the Holy Spirit.

A Life Poured Out in Service

My understanding of the priesthood has deepened, particularly through one of the books Bishop Sheen wrote on the priesthood entitled *A Priest Is Not His Own*. He stressed the fact that the priesthood of Christ is unique. Every other priest, whether pagan or Old Testament, always offered a victim apart from himself. For example, a lamb or a bullock was sacrificed, or first fruits were offered. But Bishop Sheen reminds every priest in Christ that Christ offered himself. Jesus was both Priest and Victim.

And so I have come to realize that to be a faithful priest, I too must be willing to be a "victim" with Christ. Like St. Paul, the priest must pour out his life in the service of Christ and the Church. It is both a challenge and a joy to offer priestly service to our brothers and sisters in Christ. This thought has truly been a sustaining factor in my life as a priest. Since Jesus was crucified for our sake, we must offer our lives in victimhood for his sake.

Toward the end of the homily of my ordination Mass, Bishop Sheen said, "The emotional thrill of the first Mass will leave, but not the love of being a priest—that grows as the years go on!" How prophetic he was!

The joy of being a priest can be overwhelming, as any man who loves the gift he has received will testify. (Undoubtedly, there are also days that cost a great deal in terms of sacrifice!) As I look forward to each day as a priest, I love all the various things that I may be involved in: hearing confessions, preaching, counseling, speaking at conferences, or writing books.

But if I had to pick one thing I look forward to the most, it would be the celebration of the Holy Sacrifice of the Mass. At no other moment is a priest more joined to Christ than at the Consecration of the Mass when he says the words of institution of the Eucharist over the bread and wine: "This is my Body . . . This is the cup of my Blood. . . . " We say in theology that the priest speaks *in persona Christi* ("in the person of Christ"). Though I and every other priest at the Consecration are standing at the altar, it is Christ speaking in and through us. The priest's words become Christ's words in a mysterious manner. The realization of this truth can be overwhelming.

The words of St. Padre Pio greatly inspire me. He said that when we are at the Sacrifice of the Mass, we should picture our-selves standing at the foot of the cross of Jesus next to Our Blessed

Lady, next to St. John the Beloved Disciple, and next to St. Mary Magdalene. He said that is where we really are in spirit.

It is both the great joy and awesome responsibility of a priest, then, to take the cross of Christ from Calvary and put it down in whatever city or town or village where he may be offering the Mass. As Bishop Sheen said, again in the homily at my ordination, "What Jesus did on Calvary was localized in time (two thousand years ago) and space (eight thousand miles from where I am right now). But through the Mass, Jesus made it possible for his saving death and the power of his resurrection to be present wherever his people would be gathered."

Even though every priest has to strike his breast and say *"Domine, non sum dignus"* ("Lord, I am not worthy"), what could be a greater thing to look forward to every day? Despite my unworthiness, I still recall the feeling that I had as a young six-year-old altar boy: "I want to do what the priest is doing." It is the Lord who chooses his priests! And so, a priest must always remember that he carries the treasure of the priesthood of Christ in the fragile earthen vessel of his own weak humanity.

Fr. Andrew Apostoli, CFR, is a member of the Community of the Franciscan Friars of the Renewal. Active in teaching, preaching retreats and parish missions, and giving spiritual direction, he has authored seven books and has also produced a number of television series. He is serving as vice-postulator for the Cause of Canonization for Archbishop Fulton J. Sheen.

Chapter 10

My Vision of the Priesthood

Cardinal Joseph Bernardin

Cardinal Joseph Bernardin was appointed archbishop of Chicago in 1982. His homily the evening before he was installed, delivered on August 24, 1982, to the priests of the archdiocese, contained an eloquent vision of the priesthood. An excerpt of that homily, entitled "I Am Joseph, Your Brother," is reprinted below. Cardinal Bernardin passed away on November 14, 1996, from pancreatic cancer.

Peace be with you. This is my first greeting to you, the priests who serve this local Church, the Archdiocese of Chicago. Peace be with you and all the parish communities you represent. Peace be with your families and friends. Tonight in all sincerity I want to embrace each of you in the peace of Christ. From the warm welcome you have given me, I already feel that the peace I offer rests upon you and that you embrace me in peace. The peace we share strengthens me as I begin my pastoral ministry among you.

. . . What is my vision of the priesthood? I hope to answer in word and deed over the months and years to come. I look forward to hearing your answers as well. I have been a priest for thirty years, and I still do not fully comprehend the mystery of the priesthood. But this much I do know: The priesthood is not a job. The priest is not a functionary, not a general practitioner, not a poor man's psychologist. True, many things about priestly ministry resemble a job. Priests ask, for example, "Where are you working now?" We have work schedules, organizations, a distinctive uniform. But still, the priesthood is not a job.

Here in Chicago we are blessed to have one of the largest and most diverse communities of priests in America: diocesan and religious; pastors and educators, serving inner-city, suburban, and rural communities; chaplains in hospitals and jails; those in specialized ministries; and those who serve at the Archdiocesan Pastoral Center, to name a few. As important as this diversity is, ours remains the one priesthood of Christ. We cannot measure our success and failure by the standards of the world. We must not think that moving from one post to another is "moving up or down in the Church," as if the body of Christ were a giant corporation. Whatever each of us is called to do as a priest, we are all building up the Mystical Body. All ministry is pastoral ministry. We are all laborers for the one Harvest Master.

The priesthood is a passionate commitment, a fiery-eyed vision, and an insatiable thirst for holiness and practical justice. The priest is called to be challenger, enabler, life giver, poet of life, music maker, dreamer of dreams. He must be a man of deep personal faith, conformed to Christ, a man who loves the Scriptures, draws sustenance from the sacramental life of the Church, and truly knows the community with and for whom he offers sacrifice. A priest is a man with a clear sense of his own self, one who strives to develop all his natural talents to the limit for the good of the Church. He is a man of unreasonable hopes and expectations, who takes seriously, for himself and others, the injunction to be perfect as the heavenly Father is.

Priests of this generation will see George Orwell's menacing 1984 come and go. They will witness the start of the third millennium of Christianity. Together we face a future that is familiar yet startlingly new. As we proclaim that the reign of God is at hand, none of us knows where the Church is in her pilgrimage. Some suppose she has just begun the journey, others that she is at midpoint, still others that the goal itself is in sight. We do not know. But building upon the solid achievements of the past, we must all set our faces to the future. Our lives and ministries will be the foundation stones for the Church to come.

To be good priests, we must first be good men. This requires that we seek to understand the mystery of our whole humanity. We must make provision for our physical, emotional, and psychological health. We cannot hide from life. Our vocation is not a matter of "easy hours and no heavy lifting." Only by living life in all its complexity will we be able to serve our people with compassion. Our genuine interest and authenticity should be manifest. If we are truly comfortable with ourselves and have a deep appreciation of our celibate commitment, we should not fear opening ourselves to others in love and lasting friendships. Like everyone else, the priest needs affection.

A Radical, Spiritual Commitment

Our priesthood must also be fed by an inner silence, a spiritual tranquility, public and private prayer, and an abiding joy. Without prejudice to the important social mission of the Church, the basic thrust of our efforts as priests must be spiritual. That is what is unique about our ministry. Indeed, only a radical spiritual commitment can sustain us in our efforts on behalf of the poor and downtrodden. To understand and appreciate this, we must turn to Jesus himself, seeking in him the wisdom, guidance, and strength we need to fashion our priestly ministry. Any attempt to explain the priesthood apart from the mystery of Christ and his Church is fruitless. Any attempt to tear the ministerial priesthood from its roots in Christ and in the Church will bring disillusionment and failure. The effort to explain the priesthood in purely human terms, though often well-intentioned, has in fact caused confusion and pain among the best of us. Such efforts rob the priesthood of its essentially spiritual task of reconciling all people to one another and to God through the power of Christ and the Holy Spirit.

As the Holy Father reminds us, the Eucharist is the very source of our identity as priests and the source, too, of our ministry to Christ's priestly people. In the Eucharist, God reveals who he is to us in Christ, and we reveal who we are. In liturgy we seek to be men of public prayer, men of transparent, tangible faith, in order to inspire and encourage prayer in others. We can proclaim the gospel convincingly only if we have heard its echo in the stillness of our own hearts. We can break the bread of life only if we ourselves have been broken and given, and found life in the giving. As Pope John Paul tells us: "Our whole priestly existence is and must be deeply imbued with this service, if we wish to effect in an adequate way the eucharistic sacrifice *in persona Christi*" (*Letter to All Priests of the Church, Holy Thursday*, 1979).

Liturgical spirituality is not something we can put on or take off like a chasuble. It must be real. It must flow from who we really are. It arises from an intensely intimate relationship with Jesus, a relationship which can exist and be nourished only through prayer. Like it or not, we reveal our own prayer life—or lack of it—to those we would lead in prayer.

This is why prayer cannot simply be a part of our lives. It must be everything. It must be, as Teresa of Avila writes, the heavenly rain that waters the garden of our soul. Such prayer gives meaning to our priesthood, foundation to our liturgical ministry, clarity to our pursuit of justice, and strength for our perseverance. It is the beginning of our eternal union with the Lord, who is the greatest lover we will ever know.

Chapter 11

"I Was in Prison and You Visited Me"

Fr. Paul Breau

God works in mysterious ways. Never had I thought that I would work in the penal system. But I share this part of my ministry as a priest because, during all these years, I have so much loved ministering to these men and boys. And I praise God for using me as his instrument!

I was born in 1931 in the city of Moncton, New Brunswick, Canada, into a French Acadian family, the youngest of seven children. I was ordained on the Easter Vigil in 1955, and I have worked in a variety of ministries, including serving as pastor of several large parishes and as vocation director for the diocese. As a young priest, I ministered at a camp to boys who had been in trouble with the law in some way, and I found it very hard, but perhaps that is why I now enjoy working with inmates so much. These were children from broken homes, who often had no one to care for them. The open-air camps gave them a chance to get away from the city.

My foray into prison ministry was launched twenty-five years ago, when I met a Baptist minister at the local hospital where I was assisting in pastoral care. He asked if I would work with him at a detention center in the area. The minister was not bilingual, and he was very eager to meet the needs of the French and Catholic population of boys and men. So I started going to the detention center every week to meet the inmates that needed a priest. I would also attend a meeting beforehand with staff, which gave me a chance to know more about each inmate I was about to meet.

Then in 2000, after I retired from much of my parish work, I was invited by a nun to go to the federal penitentiary in Dorchester, about eighteen miles from my home. For the last nine years, I have been going on weekends and whenever I am needed.

The Vulnerability of the Inmates

Since I have been working in these prison environments, I have changed my opinion about the men incarcerated there. Even though they have made mistakes, they are all creatures of God, loved by him and saved through him. As I've gotten to know these men, I realize that they are very vulnerable. Most of them have very sad backgrounds. They come from broken homes, were often abused by parents or neighbors, and have lived in toxic environments filled with drugs and violence. Often one or the other parent was an alcoholic. As a human being, I have pity for them.

However, as a Catholic priest, my ministry goes beyond pity. I have the opportunity to reveal to them all the love that God has for them. I also try to make them understand that there is no wrongdoing or evil they could have done that is so serious that God won't forgive them. Many of these men have no contact with God because they think that the wrong they have done is beyond forgiveness. One of my main purposes in working with them is to help them understand all the love and mercy that God has for them.

As I celebrate the holy Eucharist every Saturday at the institution, I talk a lot about the mercy and love of God for each and every one of us. I try to find examples and stories that have come from other penal institutions. I realize that I am simply an instrument in the hands of God. God the Spirit gives grace and touches the heart. With this in mind, I keep on working and let the Spirit of God touch their hearts.

Every Lent and Advent, we offer the inmates a chance to come and celebrate the Sacrament of Reconciliation in a penitential service. The lay chaplain presides over the celebration, and I hear confessions. It might surprise some to know how many men participate and how seriously they take this sacrament—God be praised!

The Meaning of the Cross

For many years, I have been giving out wooden crosses. I have my own way of doing this; I don't just pass them out randomly. The inmate has to make a request for one, and then I meet with him alone so that I can get acquainted with him. I take this occasion to explain the true meaning of the cross, and I invite the men to pray with me as I bless the cross. I also suggest to them that every night they hold the cross in their hand and thank Christ for what he has given them that day and for all the love he gave them by dying on the cross. Sometimes an inmate will ask for a cross for his friend. My answer is "Tell him to come, and I will give it to him." Some come; others refuse.

The least thing you do for these men is deeply appreciated, whether it be to give them a holy card or holy water, or to offer prayers for a sick friend or condolences for relatives or friends. Never have I been I insulted or mistreated by an inmate.

My ministry does not end with their release. Many will go back to their hometown far away in others parts of our country. But for those going to a halfway house in Moncton, I give them my phone number. If they wish to contact me, I will meet them for coffee. It gives me a chance to help them and support them in their search for work and their adaptation to their lives back on the street.

In all these years that I have been working in prison ministry, I hope that I have helped many of the men to find peace in their hearts. I pray to God that they have renewed their relationships with him. We all feel at times that the mercy of God will never extend to us. When I pray with the men individually, I always present them to God as sinners who desire to change their lives. Each soul is important to Christ and to me as well. My prayers go out for all the inmates of the institution. Whenever they need a priest, I am always available.

We know that these last years have been difficult for the Church, but I still say that the Holy Spirit is alive and well in his Church and in his people! In the 1960s and 70s, the Church witnessed new movements of the Spirit, such as Cursillo, Marriage Encounter, and Teen Encounter. I became involved in those movements, and it helped to renew my priesthood. Today I am still involved with Cursillo—I need it for my own spiritual growth.

The Lord needs fellow Christians working together to accomplish his mission. This calling comes from our baptism, when we are anointed priest, prophet, and king. We are blessed in these institutions to have laypeople coming every week to share their faith and love with these inmates. They are true witnesses to Christ to these men. We need this type of witnessing more and more in our institutions, especially with the lack of vocations.

Witnessing to Christ is not always easy, but the Holy Spirit supports me in my effort to be a good priest. I often thank the good Lord for his presence in my life every day. After fifty-four years in the priesthood, I can say that God has been with me and has helped me in every ministry that has been assigned to me. Praise to you, O Lord!

Fr. Paul Breau was born in 1931 in Moncton, New Brunswick, Canada, and was ordained on April 9, 1955. He has served as pastor of several large parishes, as vocation director for his diocese, and for the past twenty-five years, in prison ministry. He currently serves at Dorchester Penitentiary in New Brunswick as well as at Westmorland Institution, which allows inmates to live in group housing and to do their own laundry and cooking.

Chapter 12

In the Center of God's Will

Fr. Tim Vakoc, a priest of the Archdiocese of St. Paul, was serving as an army chaplain in Iraq. As he returned from saying Mass on May 29, 2004, his Humvee was hit by a roadside bomb. He suffered a brain injury and lost one eye. After numerous infections and a subsequent stroke, doctors had given up hope that he would ever recover beyond his minimally responsive state, but he began talking in October 2006. Despite other setbacks, over the next three years Fr. Vakoc continued to make progress. He died of an accidental fall on June 20, 2009, at a Minneapolis area nursing home. This homily at his funeral Mass was delivered by his friend, Fr. Stan Mader.

Thank you to all of you who are here today—family and friends; Fr. Tim's caretakers and visitors; his brother priests; military personnel; Archbishop Nienstedt and Bishop Higgins; General Rutherford; other Church leaders; and civic leaders. You honor Tim and his family and his life by being here today. And honestly, he would have loved the attention.

Tim was a man of extraordinary contradiction. He enjoyed attention, frequently mugging in photos and attracting attention, yet he was very humble. He was outrageous and sometimes embarrassingly inappropriate, but deeply prayerful and spiritual. He was an amazing collector of new gadgets and electronics, sought out creature comforts, yet was somehow very simple in how he lived. His puns were awful, and sometimes brilliant.

He loved to travel and meet new people, often using opening lines that most of us would not use with people we have known for years. Yet somehow he made friends and endeared himself to others.

He was attracted to the edges of life and adventure. I recall a video of a rafting trip he was on in Africa—rushing down a raging river with guides, making sure he was in the very front to be the first to face whatever was in store. In traveling he would just take off—going behind the Iron Curtain or into some other potentially complicated situation, simply because he had heard from someone on the train that it was worth a visit, often holding to the idea that it is easier to get forgiveness than permission.

Many of you know the exteriors of Tim's life—his early life in Robbinsdale, [Minnesota], the youngest of three children; moving to Mound in his early teens; graduating from Benilde-St. Margaret's High School, then St. Cloud State University. He was a member of the TKE fraternity and was employed by them for a few years after that as a troubleshooter, organizer, and fraternity builder before answering the call to priesthood.

After his ordination right here in St. Paul's Cathedral on May 30, 1992, he ministered at St. Charles Borromeo in St. Anthony and at St. John Neumann in Eagan. For some years he had been in chaplaincy training for the U.S. Army, and finally went into full-time army chaplaincy. His assignments included Heidelberg, Germany; then Hanau, also in Germany, where he was assigned to an aviation unit. From there he was deployed to Bosnia. Then back to Hanua, to Fort Carson in Colorado, then Fort Lewis in Washington, and from there deployment to Iraq, where we all know he was injured as a result of a roadside explosion on the eve of his twelfth anniversary as a priest. He received over a dozen ribbons, medals, and awards, including the Purple Heart. He was named distinguished alumni of both his high school and his seminary.

I traveled with him a few times—most of our seminary class was in Israel for a semester together. We were never sure whether the next Mideast crisis would be because of him or resolved by him. Later we traveled across the U.S. to Spokane, attending ordinations along the way. He got me into officer housing on a base and introduced me to incredible sights in Glacier Park, but also frustrated me by how slowly he moved in the morning.

We also spent time together in Colorado, where I saw just how much he loved being an army chaplain and how good he was at it. I know that in Bosnia and Iraq, he had to deal with injuries and deaths, and ministered to soldiers about those terrible things. He also worked with them on other topics that meant much to them: loneliness, lost opportunities, broken relationships. He developed a ministry of intentional presence among the soldiers: among them, the same but different. He was in some ways the most unmilitary and unpriestlike person I met in the seminary, but I came to appreciate him much more as a priest as I discovered that he was a prayerful, committed, spiritual, and faithful man who was able to minister very effectively to people that I could not have reached.

His Bed Was His Altar

Tim loved life, and he lived it large. Clearly, that took a turn when he was injured in Iraq. As he was being deployed to Bosnia, his sister, Anita, worried about his safety. He told her, "The safest place for me to be is in the center of God's will, and if that is in the line of fire, that is where I will be." After he was injured, Archbishop [of Military Services Edwin] O'Brien told him that he was still a priest, and now his bed would be the altar on which he would offer his sacrifice. Tim went to Iraq not for war but to provide the possibility of peace to those to whom he was called to minister. He is not a martyr; he didn't desire death. He is not a war hero—war was not what he wanted. He was a priest, and answered the call to minister in a different and powerful way to people who have close encounters with danger and death.

At funerals we are very aware of the death and resurrection of Jesus Christ, and we are reminded that we can share in it. The first reading [from Wisdom 3] assures us that the souls of the just are in the hand of God, that no torment shall touch them. In spite of appearances, they are in peace. Tim was proven as gold in the furnace. We die and rise throughout our lives—dying to bad habits to rise to healthier lives; dying to anger to rise in forgiveness; dying to sin to rise in freedom. Tim died to so many things when he was injured, but rose to a new ministry of powerful witness to the value of life . . . a new ministry of intercessory prayer—books full of intercessions that he would pray for . . . a ministry of helping people who prayed the Scriptures or the [Divine] Office with him see deeper meanings in the word . . . a ministry of listening . . . a ministry of building the great community of caregivers who learned to love one another.

In our gospel we hear the powerful story of life over death in the raising of Lazarus. We hear the statement by Mary, Lazarus' sister: "Lord, if you had been here, my brother would not have died" (John 11:21). And perhaps we question where God was five years ago—a quarter second either way, and Tim would not have been injured. Or we could ask about the many close calls with infections he had, or how he finally died—or how any of the millions through history have died from violence or accident. What was Jesus' answer? It is not about the omnipotence of God or some philosophy of life. He did what we have all done. He wept. Then he called on the Father, and called forth Lazarus from the tomb. And when Lazarus came out, Jesus said, "Untie him and let him go" (John 11:44).

Now is the time for us to let Tim go. Let him go, knowing he is in the hands of God. Let him go from the bed that has been his altar of sacrifice. Let him go, knowing that if we have died with Jesus, we shall also live with Jesus. Let him go, for he always walked into that mystery of dying and rising. Let him go, for the safest place for him is to be in the center of God's will. And it is our hope, and our belief, that that is where he is.

Chapter 13

The Hound of Heaven

Fr. Mark Ross

I can't remember a day in my life when the thought of being a priest was not in some way or other in my mind. Now that I look back on that fact, I'm astounded that I had so many doubts about becoming a priest. I doubted that God was truly calling me, and I wondered if I was consumed with a calling that I wasn't meant to have. Now I thank God that he did not give up on me. He truly is, as the famous poem says of him, the "Hound of Heaven."

My parents, who knew each other barely two months, married at seventeen, and I was born a year later. They eventually had five more children and recently celebrated their fifty-third wedding anniversary. As you might imagine, their first years were difficult. When I was four years old, a Jesuit priest, Fr. Thomas Gillin, helped my parents through that difficult period. Even though the Jesuits left our diocese within a year of my parents getting to know Fr. Gillin, their friendship endured and has continued even to this day.

Each year as I grew up, Fr. Gillin would visit my family and was a source of good counsel to my parents and us kids. His visits were a special time for the family, and sometimes I would let it be known that I was thinking of becoming a priest. He was always supportive but never pushy about the subject, which, given my penchant for not wanting to be manipulated, was the right move.

In my last year of college, I visited the vocation director of our diocese and told him of my possible calling. He ended our conversation by saying, "Now, you need to decide whether you should be a religious or a diocesan priest." I hadn't known there was a difference. It just so happened that I was reading a history of the Counter-Reformation by Henri Daniel-Rops as well as a biography of St. Ignatius of Loyola, which inspired me. I thought of Fr. Gillin and our friendship with him, and wondered if this was God's way of calling me to be a Jesuit.

After college I was accepted by the Jesuit's Southern Province and spent a short time in the novitiate in Grand Coteau, Louisiana. However, I left the novitiate about three weeks after completing the month-long Spiritual Exercises. I returned home, not knowing where to begin again. I had for my whole life felt that God was calling me to be a priest, and now it seemed that I was too unsettled and doubtful to do what I had always thought to be my destiny.

Yet within a year, I entered a diocesan seminary. In the summer months, I was assigned to a summer camp for children of the diocese. Toward the end of the summer, I was battling an intestinal bug and had lost about twenty pounds. I was also once again doubtful about whether the Lord was really calling me. Perhaps, I thought, I was just fooling myself.

"Lord, Save Me!"

Finally I decided to meet with the diocesan vocation director to tell him that I was through with the seminary. To get there, I borrowed a seminarian's car. However, as I was driving, I didn't realize that the emergency brake was on. As I took the exit off the highway going about sixty miles an hour, I began to apply the brakes. No brakes! I pumped the brakes and prayed out loud, "Lord, if you save me now, I'll go back to the seminary!" By the time the brakes did engage, I was in the middle of the road, and thankfully no cars were there to meet me. I breathed a sigh of relief and said, "Lord, you know I was just kidding!"

When I met the vocation director at the door of his residence, the first thing he said to me was "I don't know why this came to me in the mail, but it's for you." It was an invitation to the vow ceremony of the men from the Jesuit novitiate. It was sent from one of the novices, who was a friend of mine. He had heard that I was now in a diocesan seminary and had written, "Glad to hear that the 'hound of heaven' is still after you." As I read his note, I felt very conflicted, but I was determined to do what I came to do.

So I went ahead and told the vocation director that I was leaving the seminary. I remember saying to him, "I do not want to be a priest, and I ask that if I ever request to be admitted back to the seminary, you promise not to take me!" He said, "What?" I explained: "There is something either mentally or emotionally wrong with me. I know that I will most likely ask to come back, but please don't let me." The vocation director said that based on my evaluations from the seminary, he couldn't make that promise. Everything that had been written about me was positive.

For the next two years, I worked in a city on the other side of the state as a sales representative for an electrical wholesaler. True to form, within a year and a half of leaving the seminary, I was reapplying to go back. God was pulling me, but believe it or not, I was again pulling back! I still had doubts about "my calling," but I decided that I was going to stay, despite my doubts. This time I would leave only if the seminary administration told me to go home. So I was ordained a deacon, but my doubts, though they lessened, were still haunting me.

Then something unexpected happened: I was ordained a priest, and my doubts completely vanished. I was given an interior certitude that this *was* my calling. This grace has been a great source of strength and joy. The Lord, for reasons known only to him, allowed this bumpy ride, so to speak, and now has given me this unforeseen grace. I have certainly needed it!

As a side note, the priest who was the vocation director when I left after my summer assignment says he doesn't remember my request to be denied reentrance. Although he doesn't remember, I have no doubt that I said it, nor do I doubt that the "hound of heaven" is one powerful pursuer. Thanks be to God!

Fr. Mark Ross was born in Pensacola, Florida, and grew up in Augusta, Georgia. He was ordained in 1988. Since 2003, he has been blessed to serve as pastor of St. James in Savannah, which he calls "a great parish and school."

Chapter 14

The Mystery of Grace

Fr. Alfred McBride, OPraem

Although I regularly help in parishes on weekends, the principal pastoral ministry of my priesthood has been expressed in writing, lecturing, and teaching the truths of faith. This was not the result of my strategic planning, since I am not much good at it. No, I was moved forward by the blessings of God through the kindness of others. My journey was a series of graced interventions. And grace, though a mystery, is the way God works through the priesthood, as he does through any of us, whatever our vocation. One event in particular that illustrates the action of grace remains etched in my memory.

It was 1987, and the United States Conference of Catholic Bishops had invited me to write the catechesis for the upcoming pastoral visit of Pope John Paul II to America. After I was finished, I was appointed to act as a representative of the bishops to the media during his visit. I spent most of my time answering reporters' questions. Each day I also attended one of the various papal events, including Pope John Paul's visit to Hollywood. He was booked to give an address to the "movers and shakers" of the movie and television industry on their responsibilities to the public.

Three hundred guests met in the Sheraton Universal Studio Hotel in Hollywood, and we arrived one hour before the talk.

The pope was in an adjoining small theatre in the round, giving a talk to teenagers. In our room the chairs faced a wall, with a dozen TV monitors mounted near the ceiling so that we could follow the pope speaking to the youth. Instead of watching and listening, however, the movie moguls were making deals with each other and not paying much attention to the papal lecture.

When John Paul finished speaking, a young man in the adjoining theatre said, "Holy Father, we have some gifts for you. Come in, New Orleans." The voice of someone from that city responded: "Holy Father, we bring the gift of prayer for blessings on your work." The announcer continued: "Come in, St. Louis." "Holy Father, we offer you the gift of concern for the poor." "Come in, San Francisco." "Holy Father, we present you with the gift of chastity."

During this part of their program, our audience quieted down. They were apparently fascinated by what young people were saying to the pope. Lastly, the announcer said, "Holy Father, we bring you the gift of music." At that an armless young man walked to the circular stage and sat down on a chair. His name was Tony Melendez, and he had been born without arms because he had been exposed to the drug thalidomide in utero. Someone placed a guitar at his feet, and he began to play the guitar with his toes. Then he began singing a song he had composed for the pope.

At its conclusion Pope John Paul literally jumped off the platform where he had been seated and walked up to the stage, saying in his deep and mesmerizing voice, "Tony! Tony!" Then he wrapped his arms around the armless man while millions watched from around the globe. The camera scanned Tony's face and moist eyes. You could see him wondering how he could be so blessed by one of the holiest men on earth.

In our adjoining room, I could hear the silence. It was like a communal religious experience. For nearly ten minutes, no one spoke. Then the men from the U.S. Secret Service came in, announcing the immediate arrival of the pope. "Remain seated!" they commanded. But when John Paul entered, everybody stood; some climbed up on their chairs, and all applauded and cheered. Then he addressed them, and of all the speeches I heard him give on that trip, this one was the best. It was a careful and warm appeal to them to produce the finest art—art that would ennoble the human spirit and fill our world with beauty, truth, and goodness.

A Renewal of My Own Priesthood

Not only was I immensely proud of the priesthood of Pope John Paul, but I also was blessed with a renewal of my own priesthood. Through him the person of Christ shone, not only when he embraced a humble musician, but also when he joyfully extolled the real vocation of the top leaders in the world of film and television. He called them to live by the highest ideals implicit in the creative arts. No scolding. No irony. Just the truth.

It was a brief and shining moment of what dreams are made of. In the magic of those two encounters, the mystery of grace appeared. As I eavesdropped on the comments afterward, I heard bits and pieces: "inspiring" . . . "challenging" . . . "motivating." Pope John Paul showed me how a priest can bring the sacred into the most secular of environments, and do so effectively. He was like St. Paul at Athens, who had won a few converts and obtained a respectful hearing (see Acts 17:15-34). When they asked for bread, he did not give them a stone.

In my priesthood I find this to be true, whether ministering to believers or conversing with unbelievers. Every so often I hear of ways I have touched someone. "Your homily brought me back to the Church." "I have tapes of your Holy Week talks. I listen to them every year and find new meanings." "I want to get adults to read your history of the Church." One friend wrote, "Thanks for being the wind beneath my wings." I owe all this to God's merciful love.

I wrote this reflection on my priestly calling just two days before the fifty-sixth anniversary of my ordination on June 20, 1953. I remember how hot and humid it was, 95 degrees outside and no air conditioning. At my first Mass the following day, as I was giving my first blessings, I was surprised, moved, and humbled by the tears of many, especially Mr. McNulty, the man who wrote the St. Vincent de Paul checks for the poor, from which my family benefited during the toughest part of the Depression.

I don't tend to dwell on the difficult days of my priesthood, other than to note that God did not spare me the cross. He gave me a generous dose of setbacks, but nothing my shoulders could not carry as long as I had his grace and love. Thanks, God. I love you. I love our people.

Fr. Alfred McBride, OPraem, is the house superior for the Norbertines at St. Joseph Priory, De Pere, Wisconsin. He is a writer and lecturer and the author of many books, including his latest, Praying with Jesus and the Saints.

Chapter 15

Healing Broken Hearts

Fr. Jude Winkler, OFM Conv

I believe that if you were to ask most priests about their early ideas of what the priesthood would be like, they would talk about how they pictured themselves celebrating the Mass. I can remember some moments when those thoughts crossed my mind as well. I even remember as a child "playing" the priest at Mass. But today my priesthood is much more tied to another sacrament: Reconciliation.

When I was in high school and trying to decide what to do with the rest of my life, I had two options that seemed enticing. I could be a biochemist or I could be a priest. I knew that a biochemist could invent a new type of food and nourish those who were starving to death. A priest could heal people's hearts. It was difficult to decide which mission was the more important.

The night that I had to decide which of these alternatives to pursue, I lay down in bed and listened to an audiotape of a rock opera, *Jesus Christ Superstar*. I was so moved by what I heard that the next day, I turned down the various scholarships I had been offered and resolved to become a Franciscan priest.

I did my basic studies in our college seminary in Massachusetts, and was sent on to Rome for three years of theology and then four years of biblical studies. After my first four years of studies, I was ordained a priest.

While in Rome I helped out on the weekends in a poor storefront church in the outskirts of the city. One Saturday evening I was getting ready to celebrate Mass. Looking out to the congregation, I saw eight ladies and one man in church. (The man who had stumbled in happened to be drunk, and by the end of the "Lord, have mercy," the ladies had escorted him out.)

I asked each of the ladies if she would be willing to do the readings, and only one agreed. I found out later that the others were illiterate. Well, this particular lady did a fine job.

Immediately after Mass the pastor rushed into the sacristy and told me that I could never ask this woman to read again. I asked him why, pointing out that she had done a great job. He responded that she had just returned to church. Up until a few months ago, she had lived as a public sinner. Now, it wouldn't have bothered me if she had read again, but it would have scandalized the others in church, so I agreed.

A couple of minutes later, the woman entered the sacristy and asked to see me the following Saturday. We made an appointment for five in the afternoon. Since it was Rome, she showed up the next Saturday at five thirty. I asked her what she wanted to talk about, and she said she wanted to go to confession. I asked her if she knew how to do it, and she said no, that it had been a while.

After we made the sign of the cross, I asked her what she meant by "a while." Was it two months or maybe two years? She answered, "Oh no, it's been fifty-seven years." I gulped and said that was quite a while. I asked her what had made her want to go to confession that day. She answered, "Last Friday night I had a dream that a man dressed in white (my alb) would ask me to preach in front of the church." (She really didn't understand the difference between reading and preaching.) Whoever asked her to "preach," she was to go to confession to that man. A shiver ran up my spine. I was the only priest at that parish who didn't know her past, the only one who would have asked her to read. God had pushed us together that powerfully.

I now preach up to thirty parish missions each year. One of the gifts I can offer is to be an outside priest to whom people can go to confession, especially if they haven't been for a while or are too embarrassed to go to their own priests. One lady said to me, "Father, I was waiting for an old, deaf priest, but since you're leaving on Friday, you're the next best thing."

Reborn in Christ

I always offer time each day for confession. Even in parishes where very few go normally, I usually end up with huge lines. If I am in the confessional from four to five in the afternoon, the first day I will have about forty-five minutes of confessions. The second day, it's up to an hour. The third day, it is an hour and a half. By the fourth day, it is not unusual to have two and a half hours of confessions.

I can't describe how peaceful people look when they have not been to confession for twenty or thirty or forty years, and they finally find the courage to begin again. Or maybe they have gone to confession regularly, and they know they held back one serious sin many years ago because they were afraid that Monsignor would recognize their voice. When they finally let go of that sin, it's as if they were reborn.

What a privilege it is for me to be able to listen to their confessions. They are often worried that I will look down on them because of what they have confessed, but for me it's like going on retreat. I marvel at their openness and vulnerability. I am filled with a sense of compassion when I listen to their struggles. It fills me with awe and calls me to my own conversion.

I am so grateful to God that I have been given this ministry. I really do feel that my priesthood has been an opportunity to heal broken hearts.

Fr. Jude Winker is a member of the St. Anthony Province of the Conventual Franciscan Friars. He is involved full-time in the evangelization ministry of the Companions of St. Anthony, preaching throughout the U.S. and writing articles and books about Sacred Scripture. Born in Buffalo, New York, in 1953, he was ordained in 1981 and is currently stationed at St. Joseph Cupertino Friary in Ellicott City, Maryland.

Chapter 16

Witnessing to Jesus

Fr. Guido Gockel, MHM

I have served as a missionary priest in many different places across the globe. Yet even though I am an ordained priest, I believe that I have no greater calling than to live my Christian vocation.

In fact, the greatest call for anyone is to be a Christian, to live in union with Jesus. When we allow our minds and hearts to be transformed by this union, we become like him in mind and heart. At baptism we are anointed priest, prophet, and king. As priest, we offer ourselves in sacrifice for others. As prophet, we live as witnesses to faith, hope, and love (with words if necessary, as St. Francis said). And as king, we allow love to order our relationships with others—for that's where heaven and eternity begin. It is my joy and privilege to live this Christian vocation, following Jesus' call to "Go out to all the nations!" (see Matthew 28:19).

My preparation for my missionary and priestly life began in the 1960s, during and after the Second Vatican Council. It was a period of turmoil, when the world and the Church began a new period of history in what we would now call a globalized world. The changes implemented after Vatican II had been difficult for many people, including my dad. When I was preparing to be ordained and celebrate my first Mass, my brother and sisters asked me to say it in Latin so that Dad could hear me say *"hoc est enim corpus meum"* ("This is my body").

Reluctantly, I gave in. After Mass I gave my parents my first priestly blessing, and my father embraced me, saying, "Latin really isn't for our time any more." In retrospect my father's words were prophetic. Little did I know then the many languages I would have to learn to preach the word of God, including the "language" of the Holy Spirit!

My first missionary assignment was in the idyllic primitive conditions of the jungle of Sarawak among the Sebob, Kenyah, Kayan, Iban, and nomadic Penan peoples of Borneo, Malaysia. Traveling by longboat, I went on two- or three-week safari trips to visit people in the many longhouses (villages on stilts) built along a muddy, meandering river and its tributaries, teeming with fish and reptiles. Youthful, inexperienced, and full of enthusiasm, I learned languages, taught catechism, celebrated the sacraments, and built a little clinic. Although the mission lacked such basics as water, electricity, and privacy, I enjoyed it. I was a missionary in the "old time" sense of the word.

Enflamed with God's Love

But in this missionary environment, I was being witnessed to as well. As yet the necessary transformation of my intellectual formation had not reached my heart. It was in Borneo that a group of young people witnessed to God's love and prayed with me for the "baptism of the Holy Spirit," filling my heart with a deep sense of God's love. Thus enflamed with God's love and with renewed priestly zeal, I began to introduce the charismatic renewal to my parish and the diocese.

During this time, many who had received the baptism in the Holy Spirit felt called to form lay communities to help support one another in living the Christian life. A wise elderly Chinese priest advised me to learn about these communities. With the approval of my superior, I literally left everything and spent two years in the U.S. in training and formation. Then I became a leader in a community in Brussels and helped start new communities in Germany, Poland, and other parts of Europe. It was a time of tremendous growth at all levels of my life, which I would have been very happy to continue.

But eleven years later, I found myself suddenly battling an almost unshakable desire to go back to Borneo. It seemed to me like a temptation. Imagine my surprise when my superior called me out of the blue and begged me to go back to Sarawak! Once again leaving all behind, I returned to the Miri diocese there.

It was a great joy to see that the "colonial" church of European missionaries had become a local church with an indigenous bishop who, with all the local priests, had become deeply involved in the charismatic renewal. It was a tremendous privilege for me to be asked by the bishop to return and serve the diocese in a variety of functions—from parish priest to rector of the cathedral, from teacher of catechism and catechists to forming parish councils and liturgical ministries and giving retreats. Unfortunately, this beautiful time also came to an end, as the Malaysian government restricts residential visas to ten years.

It wasn't clear what I would do next, but I had come to know and respect the Pontifical Mission for Palestine while on a pilgrimage to the Holy Land, and I asked to be assigned to this organization of the Holy See. I was subsequently invited and appointed to become director of its office in Jerusalem.

Reflecting on the Mission of Jesus

The seven years that followed were like a golden era in my life. I felt excited about the pastoral and humanitarian aid work we were doing, and I especially relished the opportunity because in Jerusalem—this is the effect the city has on you—I was able to reflect on the great truths of our faith. As I meditated on Jesus' suffering and death, culminating in his cry on the cross, "My God, my God, why have you forsaken me?" (Matthew 27:46), I came to experience that Jesus' whole mission is summed up in his desire to be present in the deepest darkness of our hearts and lives, exactly when we feel abandoned by God. In the midst of the *Intifada* (the Palestinian uprising), the words of St. Paul that nothing can separate us from the love of God (Romans 8:39)— not war, sin, or death—became a reality in my life. Peace, which only God can give, came into my heart, with the assurance that "all is well" in God's hands.

Five years ago I was reassigned to the administrative headquarters of the Pontifical Mission in New York, working with the Catholic Near East Welfare Association, which is involved in the larger humanitarian and pastoral outreach to the homelands of the Eastern churches—India, Ethiopia, Eritrea, the Middle East, and Eastern Europe.

Having served in so many countries, painstakingly learning languages that weren't even written, I have witnessed an unheard-of Christianization of peoples, cultures, and languages through the outpouring of the Holy Spirit. Imagine: illiterate people, who remained unbaptized because they couldn't learn the *Pater Noster* by heart, experiencing Pentecost! "Each one heard them speaking in the native language of each" (Acts 2:6, NRSV). I have witnessed the Spirit blowing where he wills, making all things new *if*, like Peter, we leave our boats and walk on the water toward Jesus.

Missionaries, as they existed in colonial times, are becoming fewer and fewer. Should I—should we—be concerned? No! God's Spirit has filled the hearts of huge numbers of lay men and women with the same fire. I rejoice that the missionary zeal is no longer confined to members of missionary societies, but has stirred the hearts of many people in response to the Second Vatican Council's understanding of the Church as missionary. I feel very thankful that I was able to plant a missionary seed in Sarawak and many other countries in the world, and I now rejoice that it is bearing fruit. Imagine: in Sarawak, the work of missionaries who had actively worked and toiled for over a century is now suddenly bearing fruit, as a thousand adults ask for baptism every Easter!

It is great to be a missionary, to call people out of the romanticism of the past to embrace courageously the uncertainties of the future, for the Lord has planned for us a future full of hope (Jeremiah 29:11).

Fr. Guido was born in Tilburg, Holland, in 1944 and was ordained a Mill Hill Missionary on June 29, 1969. (The Mill Hill Missionaries were founded in England in 1866.) His missionary work has taken him around the world. He has served as director of the Pontifical Mission for Palestine, and is currently undersecretary general of the Catholic Near East Welfare Association in New York.

Chapter 17

The Priest and the Ministry of the Word

Fr. Daniel J. Harrington, SJ

The old saying that "if you love what you are doing, you will never work a day in your life" certainly applies to me. It has been my privilege, as a Jesuit for more than fifty years and a priest for almost forty years, to immerse myself in the study of the Bible—its ancient languages, forms of expression, cultural settings, and theological significance. For forty years I have been able to write about, research, and preach on what is aptly called the word of God. It has all been a joy.

The best advice anyone ever gave me came from a Jesuit dean many years ago. He said, "You should continue on in Scripture. It's the coming field." He was correct. In my studies I had the best teachers and scholars of their generation in the Society of Jesus and at Harvard University, the Hebrew University, and the École Biblique in Jerusalem. These great teachers and productive scholars approached Scripture with respect and humility. Here I want to reflect on how Scripture has personally affected me and my vocation as a priest. I will do so with reference to three biblical texts that have meant much to me along the way.

The Call

"Then the LORD *said to him [Moses], 'Who gives speech to mortals? . . . Is it not I, the* LORD?'" (Exodus 4:11, NRSV)

As a boy I stuttered. I still do at times. I had read somewhere that Moses stuttered, and so I found the relevant passage in the Bible, in Exodus 3–4. This is the account of the call of Moses to lead God's people out of slavery in Egypt. One of Moses' objections is that "I am slow of speech and slow of tongue" (4:10, NRSV). God's answer is that God is the one who gives speech to mortals.

Reading this biblical account not only gave me encouragement and hope but also introduced me to the biblical phenomenon of encounter with God and vocation. And then I discovered the many other "call" narratives in the Bible with regard to the prophets, Mary, Jesus' first disciples, and the apostle Paul. The seed of my vocation to be a Jesuit priest was planted in reading and reflecting on the call of Moses.

The Word

"You accepted it not as a human word but as what it really is, God's word, which is also at work in you believers." (1 Thessalonians 2:13, NRSV)

These words from Paul come from the earliest complete document in the New Testament. Here Paul indicates that the word of God—in this case the good news about Jesus' life, death, and resurrection (also known as the gospel and the paschal mystery)—is something "living and active, sharper than any two-edged sword"

(Hebrews 4:12, NRSV). In Paul's letters the primary form of ministry is the ministry of the word.

When, in the sixteenth century, the first members of the Society of Jesus tried to express what they wanted to do for the world and the Church, they decided on the phrase "the ministry of the word." This expression has deep biblical roots. Moses, the prophets, Jesus, and Paul all were ministers of the word. As their religious order took shape, the early Jesuits gave content to that phrase, not only in their teaching, preaching, and writing, but also in their scientific research (especially astronomy) and in linguistics (as they brought the gospel to peoples in distant lands).

I entered the Society of Jesus in 1958 at the age of eighteen. I often thank God that I found the right place for me to be a priest. I would not have been as happy or done as well as a parish priest or as a contemplative. Rather, I believe that God called me to be what is the Jesuit ideal—a contemplative in action. My "action" has taken the forms of study, teaching, research, writing, editing, community life, ecumenical and interreligious dialogue, and formation of students for ministry in the Church (along with a good deal of parish work and contemplation).

The Model

"Unlike the other high priests, he [Jesus] has no need to offer sacrifices days after day, first for his own sins, and then for those of the people; this he did once for all when he offered himself." (Hebrews 7:27, NRSV)

In the New Testament, only the Letter to the Hebrews describes Jesus as a priest. Indeed, the author of Hebrews freely admits that according to Old Testament standards, Jesus could not have been a priest because he was not from the tribe of Levi (7:13-14). However, he portrays Jesus as the great high priest because he willingly offered himself as the perfect (that is, truly effective) sacrifice for the sins of humankind. Jesus was both the sacrifice and the priest who offered the sacrifice.

Thus, Jesus founded a new priesthood rooted in the paschal mystery. As the priesthood developed in the early Christian centuries, it combined many different biblical strands: the Old Testament priesthood, the prophets, the first followers of Jesus, the apostles, and the bishops, elders, and deacons of the early communities. But the foundation and model must always be the person of Jesus and his saving death and resurrection. Recognition of this basic biblical insight can keep priests on course and help them deal with the obstacles, frustrations, and sufferings that come when life does not seem to be going their way.

Priests need support and encouragement from God's people. This can come in simple ways. Several years ago I was conducting a week-long workshop on the Book of Revelation. Near the end, a woman approached me and said, "I hope you realize that you are doing exactly what you should be doing." What I was doing was exercising my Jesuit priesthood as a minister of the word. I did know that I was doing was what I should be doing. But I was greatly encouraged by this woman's words, and have treasured them ever since.

Daniel Harrington, SJ, was born in Arlington, Massachusetts, in 1940 and was ordained on June 5, 1971. He is a renowned biblical scholar and the author of more than forty books on Scripture. He teaches at the Boston College School of Theology and Ministry, and has been the editor of New Testament Abstracts *since 1972.*

Chapter 18

God Is Full of Surprises!

Fr. Peter L. Smith

Our God is a God of surprises. Sometimes he leads us to places we would never have expected to go. When I look back on my life, I never thought that I'd become a priest. But as Scripture says, with the Lord nothing is impossible.

I was born and raised in Pietermaritzburg in South Africa, the oldest of six children in a family in which faith was very much a part of our life. We prayed together, were very involved in our parish, and had family and friends who were priests and religious. Despite this upbringing, however, I never contemplated being a priest. My plan was to graduate from business school and then law school, and then join my dad's law firm as a business lawyer. I also planned to get married and have a family, and I was in a relationship that looked as if it could end in marriage.

A Vivid Experience of Christ

But I hadn't counted on what God was going to do in my life. Just before my twenty-first birthday, I had a profound and vivid experience of Christ. I don't like to call it a conversion, as I was a faithful Catholic at the time, but it was something of a deeper conversion. Jesus became very vividly and personally real to me. I responded by asking him to be part of my life in this way thereafter. I was also convicted to seek a greater empowering of the Holy Spirit in my life, which I also experienced in a very personal and real way. I began praying each day. Both Scripture and the Mass became alive to me like never before.

As I grew in my faith life, I realized that I had made all these plans for my life, which were good, but I had never sought God's direction or guidance regarding them. So I began to pray, asking God to either confirm my choices or to guide me as he wanted. In my last year in business school, the Lord very clearly and directly invited me to consider being single for him. Several months later I discerned the Lord inviting me to consider a future that didn't involve working as a lawyer in my father's law firm. What that was, I didn't know. But after much prayer, reflection, and spiritual direction, I chose to accept these invitations. Finally, in my last semester at law school, I discerned the Lord inviting me to visit a community in the U.S. Needless to say, that really surprised me!

So a few months later, after graduating from law school, I left South Africa for the U.S. I didn't know it then, but I was to spend only nine months of the next twenty-six years back in my homeland. The community I was visiting was one of the lay communities that had developed out of the Catholic charismatic renewal. I soon discovered that in addition to the families and singles, there was a brotherhood and a sisterhood for those who had discerned a call to live together in dedicated celibacy. After almost a year, I went on a retreat with the men from this brotherhood and then moved into the house where they lived. For the past twenty-five years, I have lived as a brother with them.

Some years later the possibility of ordination opened up for the men in our brotherhood, which would allow us to still live in community and at the same time be diocesan priests. When Archbishop Francis George, then of Portland, Oregon, agreed to recognize us canonically, we moved to Portland, and several of us entered the seminary there.

The next five years passed quickly, and before I knew it, in June 2001, I was being ordained. At the "young" age of forty-three, and seventeen years after leaving my homeland, I was a priest. The fact that I was older and had life experience has been a great blessing for me in my pastoral ministry responsibilities. The way I was raised in my family and the years of formation, life, and service in my community all added to what I received in the seminary and through mentor priests in the archdiocese.

I have to say that I love being a priest. I am fortunate that I live with two other priests and a brother from my community. We pray together, have meals together, and share life in community. It's a great blessing and support. A solid prayer life, individually and communally, and good supportive relationships have strengthened my priestly life and ministry. I also have a very good spiritual director who, in his kind but firm way, helps me cooperate with what God is doing in my life and holds me accountable. My confessor is an older priest who has served in many and varied ways in the Church and has also been something of a mentor for me.

The Power of God and the Sacraments

One of the things I look forward to as a priest is preaching and teaching. We as Catholic do not always understand, appreciate, and connect with the spiritual presence and power of God that are present in our sacraments and in the life of the Church. Too often I see Catholics who have been sacramentalized and ritualized, but who have not been effectively evangelized through these actions. For whatever reason, they have not connected with God in a personal or communal way in their experience of the sacraments and Church life. Having had the sacraments come alive for me, and experiencing the living and vivifying power of God in them, I want others to know and experience God similarly in their lives of faith.

I also relish the opportunities to pray with people in different situations. As a priest, you see people at many unguarded moments in their lives. (Of course, they get to see us that way at times too.) When people are suffering or struggling with issues and sin, when they are about to move on to the next step in their lives, we are often privy to and part of these moments. Sometimes it is very humbling; other times it can be very inspiring. In all those moments, if the right and appropriate opportunity presents itself, I ask people if they want me to pray with them. I have never had people turn down that offer. Perhaps they were just being nice to me, but nonetheless, God still works in those situations, sometimes in amazing ways. Enabling people to open their lives more fully to God's transforming power is one of the best ways I can help them.

On one occasion I was at a parishioner's home for dinner with about fifteen other people. The husband asked me to keep his wife in my prayers, as her one good eye was now deteriorating through macular degeneration, as her other eye had already done. I asked if we could pray with her after dinner, and they agreed. So at the end of a delightful evening, we gathered together. The wife sat in a chair, and I asked everyone else to lay hands on her. Then I led a simple prayer asking God to heal her eye. Several other people asked for prayer, and we prayed with them too. Later I found out that the wife's macular degeneration had stopped. It also turned out that one of the other guests who had asked for prayer was a Mormon, and was so moved by what she had experienced that she entered the RCIA program in a nearby parish.

Inspired by the Faith of Others

I am always inspired and moved when people come to the sacraments with a deep faith. Recently I was privileged to be part of a wedding in which the bride and groom and their families and many of their friends were Catholics with vibrant and living faith. Their wedding was more like a family reunion, with the Lord in the middle of it. Not only were people celebrating the wedding, but they were celebrating what the Father had done in this young man and young woman, and what he was doing and going to do in their married life.

Some years ago I celebrated a funeral Mass for a middle-aged woman who had died of cancer, leaving behind a husband and several young children. Both she and her husband had a strong and mature faith. The Mass was packed with mourners, and the funeral procession stretched for blocks. Yet the Mass was not somber. It was a recognition of all God had done in her and through her, and how she was the person we all knew and admired, in great part because of the Lord in her life. All too often we miss this truth. Her husband made this clear when he shared some brief words of remembrance. When we had completed the graveside service, instead of leaving, people remained for quite some time, praying quietly and then singing hymns and some of the woman's favorite religious songs. It was a tragedy, yet faith and hope shone through it all. What a wonderful witness it was!

God may have other surprises in store for me. I do know that when we open our lives to God's transforming presence and power, he may lead us to places and have us do things we never dreamed of—perhaps even leaving home, family, and country to join a community and become a priest far, far away. And if he can do that with me, think of the awesome things he can do with you!

Fr. Peter Smith was born and raised in South Africa. A member of the Brotherhood of the People of Praise community since 1983, he was ordained to the priesthood in June 2001. He has earned degrees in theology from Mount Angel Seminary and the Pontifical University San Anselmo in Rome as well as a canon law licentiate from Catholic University in Washington, D.C. In 2006 he became pastor of St. Rose of Lima Parish in Portland and also serves as a judge on the Portland Archdiocesan Tribunal.

Chapter 19

The Joy of Presiding at the Eucharist

Msgr. John Steiner

Several years ago, at a meeting of the priests of our diocese, one of the priests objected to the pious exhortation that is given to priests to celebrate the Eucharist each day. "When I have celebrated 365 Masses during the year, can I be judged to have done my part?" he asked. In fact, no one really believes that Eucharistic faith can be measured by some kind of accounting.

But for many priests, the "multiplication" of Masses is the blessing and curse of the priesthood. A weekend may mean celebrating anywhere from six to eight Masses, and in some cases, even more. How can a priest come to the altar in the service of God's people with continuing joy in his heart?

Yet in the forty years I have been a priest, I am most affirmed when people thank me for presiding at the Eucharist. The preamble to the General Instruction of the Roman Missal (GIRM) provides one of the guiding pillars of my life as a priest:

> The nature of the ministerial priesthood proper to a Bishop and a priest, who offer the Sacrifice in the person of Christ and who preside over the gathering of the holy people, is evident in the form of the rite itself, by reason of the more prominent place and office of the priest. (4)

We are what we do. "Understand, therefore, what you do and imitate what you celebrate" (a bishop's words at the ordination of priests). Presiding at the Eucharist is the heart and center of what it means to me to be a priest. When I come before a community of believers, I feel compelled by the gift that has been given to me to make their experience of Eucharist the most vital part of their day. In word and sacrament, God places my gifts and talents on the line in this unique moment for this gathering of the faithful.

The People of God and the Prayer of the Church

The most significant directive in the GIRM, in my mind, is one that has received little reflection by most celebrants at the altar. It is a fantastic invitation to me as a priest to reach out in service and joy to the people who have come to the altar:

It is also up to the priest, in the exercise of his office of presiding over the gathered assembly, to offer certain explanations that are foreseen in the rite itself. Where it is indicated in the rubrics, the celebrant is permitted to adapt them somewhat in order that they respond to the understanding of those participating. However, he should always take care to keep to the sense of the text given in the Missal and to express them succinctly. The presiding priest is also to direct the word of God and to impart the final blessing. In addition, he may give the faithful a very brief introduction to the Mass of the day (after the initial Greeting and before the Act of Penitence), to the Liturgy of the Word (before the readings), and to the Eucharistic Prayer (before the Preface), though never during the Eucharistic Prayer itself; he may also make concluding comments to the entire sacred action before the dismissal. (31)

The instruction uses a rather weak English phrase to describe this role of presiding: "a very brief introduction." The Latin text really says something different: *brevissimis verbis, introducere fideles in Missam diei.* My translation: "with very brief words to lead the faithful into the Mass of the day." As a priest, my special experience is to lead the people of God into an experience of this day's celebration of the Holy Mass, to lead them to hear and ponder and be inspired by the word of God, and finally and most significantly in my mind, to lead them into the spirit and mystery of the great prayer of thanksgiving.

I supposed that, in summary, one could say that as a priest, it is my awesome experience to engage with the people of God in the prayer of the Church. When the voice of the Church explodes within the gathering of the assembly, my work is done. "Let us pray with confidence in the words our Savior gave us. . . . Our Father . . . " When the Church prays, Christ is present and alive in our world.

If there was one outcome of the Second Vatican Council that was the hand of God in my life, it was the revised Lectionary of 1969. The new Lectionary made it so very clear that the Church can encounter the living word of God in the celebration of the liturgy. I am blessed to preside at the living proclamation of the word. It has been my joy and the enthusiasm of each day and each season to share the dynamic word of God with the gathered assembly. Sure, it has meant preparing to preach and teach and make the reading of the word meaningful and alive. But that work has placed the word of God into the very fabric of my being. Neither the word of God nor the prayer of the Church belongs as a dead letter on a printed page. Proclamation is an exercise of setting the Spirit free.

A Thankful Man and a Thankful Church

"Let us give thanks to the Lord our God." In recent years, I have used this three-part dialogue as the introduction to many occasional prayers, especially the blessing of community meals. The role of presiding at the Eucharist has made me a thankful man serving a thankful Church. I want to pause and reflect about what I am thankful for.

I am thankful for the awesome gift of life. There is nothing more significant than being alive. The Spirit of God, the breath of God, is totally a gift. To be alive is the greatest of mysteries. I am fascinated by my own breath—even though it is getting shorter these days.

I am thankful for my family and my community. I have never been left alone. I was privileged to spend many wonderful years with my father. He was ninety-six years old when he died. I can think of no greater gift than to be an appreciative son. We are all children of God, sisters and brothers to one another.

I am thankful for the gift of faith. By themselves life and family are meaningless, but with the joy of the mystery of revelation, they are filled with glorious meaning and joy. My priesthood has centered around this search for meaning. It is my joy to point out that meaning to others. When my sisters and brothers in the family of the Church are enthusiastic about the meaning and purpose of their lives, the Church is alive. Christ speaks to a world easily captured in darkness a message of light and hope.

"Do you clearly understand what you are undertaking?" Each time I baptize a baby, I shake my head at the ritual yes of unsuspecting parents. This question should be asked of those being ordained bishops, priests, and deacons as well. We are called to "parent" the Church born from the side of Christ. It is messy business. It is certainly an awesome calling. And although it comes at a precious price, it is filled with much joy.

Msgr. John M. Steiner is a priest native to the Diocese of Spokane. Ordained in 1969, he has worked as a pastor, teacher, and diocesan administrator. At present he is a vicar general in the Diocese of Spokane and pastor of St. Mary's Parish in Spokane Valley, Washington.

Chapter 20

Fanning the Flame of God's Love

Fr. Aaron Pirrera, OSB

When I think about the gift of the priesthood, I am reminded of a movie I saw many years ago. I don't recall its title, but it was a story of a prehistoric society. Two tribes had been fighting, and the winners were carrying off the women of the other tribe. One man dropped a woman and then picked up a glowing ember from a fire and placed it in a container. The first night after the battle, one of the captive women showed the victors the virtue of a fire on a cold night. It now became the job of the man who had found the ember to keep it glowing so that at the end of each night, there could be a fire.

To me, this is what it means to be a priest. It means to take that ember of God's love and keep it burning, not only in my own heart, but in the hearts of all with whom I come into contact.

Even as a young boy, I felt that God had fanned into flame a burning desire within me to become a priest. It was the only thing I ever thought about—and it certainly helped that I was encouraged by my teachers. In high school I was fairly certain that I would enter the seminary or join a religious congregation after graduation. Although I had the feeling that my parents would not be happy with that decision, I couldn't help believing that they would give me their blessing, since it was all I had ever talked about doing.

However, when I broke the news to my parents, they said that I was too young to make such a momentous decision. I was to go to college and "get that behind me." Those were the turbulent years of the sixties, and over those four long years, I started to cool toward the idea of a religious vocation. Soon after graduation I signed up for the Peace Corps and spent two years teaching in Eritrea. These were exciting years, filled with adventure and travel. Then, after my service in the Peace Corps, I taught in a public school in Iowa. Little did I know that this setting would be the catalyst for me to pursue a religious vocation.

Entering the teachers' lounge one day, I spied a Catholic newspaper. In it was an article about a monastery in Arkansas celebrating the one hundredth anniversary of its foundation. Perhaps the smoldering embers were being fanned again, if not for the priesthood, then at least for the religious life. Secretly hoping that it would be the most horrible place on earth in which to spend the rest of my life, I made arrangements for a visit.

Ten months later I was donning the tunic of a candidate for Subiaco Abbey, that very monastery. I liked the community, the setting, and the ministry. After all, I was a teacher, and the abbey had a high school attached to it. Because of my age—I was now in my late thirties—I was at peace with the idea of being a teaching brother and not a priest.

However, after formation and first vows, the abbot called me in and suggested that I study for the priesthood. I was emphatic about having lost my desire to do so. I would be forty years old before ordination, and I didn't relish the idea of studying with a group of younger men. He told me that he was considering sending me to Rome to study at the Collegio Beda, a seminary for older men. So I went to Rome, and after the prescribed years of study, I was ordained a priest for Subiaco Abbey in the Diocese of Little Rock, Arkansas.

A Priest for All People

Even after my ordination, I really wasn't able to see myself as a priest for a time, but rather, I saw myself as a monk. Of course, this is the ideal of a Benedictine vocation. However, after I served for several years as novice master, I began to understand my role as a Benedictine monk-priest. Then I was given the assignment of overseeing our guest house and retreat center. It was a great opportunity to come into contact with people from all walks of life. Being on call 24/7, I learned what it meant to be a priest to all people—not just to members of the community, but also to retreatants and folks who just stopped by because they wanted, or needed, to talk to a priest.

I also realized that ordination was not the end of my spiritual journey but only the beginning of it. As I directed retreats, gave spiritual direction, and heard confessions, I became more aware of my own sins and selfishness. I honestly believe that I learned something about myself from every encounter I had with a guest at the retreat center.

Sometimes I found it difficult to understand why people approached me to ask for advice. I often felt unqualified and was tempted to tell them to call someone else. What an eye-opener it was every time someone returned years later to say thank you for whatever I had said or the advice I had given. Often I couldn't even remember that person, let alone what I had told him or her!

During my life as a Benedictine monk-priest, I have had many great experiences and joys. Two stand out particularly in my mind.

Anyone who has ever spent time in a religious community knows that there is always one person who is troublesome and difficult to live with. One day such a brother came to me with a young woman who claimed that she was possessed by the devil. It was late at night, and I was tired—I had been preparing conferences for an upcoming retreat. The brother told me about the woman's predicament and asked me to pray over her. I wasn't sure if this was her idea or his.

We went to the chapel, and using holy water, I wet my hands and placed them on her head. I remembered having read about the "binding prayer." I recited it, keeping my hands on her head. As I prayed, her head became as hot as fire, and she began to moan and then let out a shriek. Well, needless to say, I was speechless. Almost ten years later, the woman appeared at my door to thank me for saving her life, because if that particular brother had not brought her to me, she was going to commit suicide.

On another occasion after I became pastor of the abbey parish, there was a knock at the rectory door. A woman stood there in tears and said she needed help. Since we have many transient people coming through the area, my first thought was "How much is this going to cost me?" She came in and told me that she was pregnant and was being encouraged to have an abortion by the baby's father and her friends. She hadn't yet told her family about the pregnancy. After hours of talking and praying together, she left. I thought this was the end of it. She would make up her mind and get on with her life. About a year later, she was at my door again, this time to introduce me to her baby boy. With tears in her eyes, she thanked me for the time I had spent with her.

I have to pray often and hard to be able to be all things to all people. Some want a friend, some want an advisor, some want a spiritual director, and some want nothing more than to sit down and shoot the breeze over a cool beer. I have to be a man of prayer in order to be open and available. This means sometimes forgetting how tired I am, when I secretly wish that this person would hurry up and leave. It means saying things that some people don't want to hear: you are too young to get married; you need to stop your drinking; you need to pray. It means fanning the ember of faith, hope, and charity into a flaming fire in my community and parish.

Fr. Aaron Pirrera, OSB, was born in Chicago in 1944. After serving in the Peace Corps and teaching in Iowa public schools, he entered Subiaco Abbey in Arkansas in 1978, and was ordained to the priesthood in August 1985. He is presently serving as pastor of St. Benedict Church in Subiaco.

Chapter 21

Caring for the Promised Land

Fr. Jim Hewes

When I was a seminarian, one of our professors quoted the theologian Karl Barth, who said that Christians need to have a Bible in one hand and a newspaper in the other. I always remembered that quote, but its truth came home to me one day ten years ago when I came across a short newspaper article.

The article said that thirty-one people had been killed in the Philippines by an avalanche from a huge mountain of garbage. In fact, as I discovered later, more than 250 people had been killed and 300 families had been left homeless.

I was stunned. I can't remember anything affecting me so much in my priesthood. I simply couldn't imagine that people were living among garbage and then being killed by it! I had never in my life heard of such inhumane living conditions. What I learned soon after astounded me even more: 140,000 people were living in these deplorable conditions, in what is called the Payatas Community, located in Quezon City outside Manila. (Ironically, Payatas means "promised land.") Whole families made their "living" from scavenging through the seven-story mountain of debris. We read sad stories all the time in the newspaper, but this one I could not get out of my mind.

God's Deeper Plan

At the time I had been assigned to St. John/St. Patrick Parish, located in Clyde and Savannah in rural upstate New York. My mother was in her eighties then, and living alone, about an hour away from my assignment. I was not enthusiastic about serving at a parish that was such a distance from her. My apprehension only increased when my mother was diagnosed with cancer again. In the same period of time, my only sibling, my older brother, Dave, who was Mom's main caregiver, was diagnosed with terminal cancer. It was a difficult time during this assignment. But God had a deeper plan.

While I continued to carry out my responsibilities as pastor, I decided that I needed to do something to try to help the people in this Filipino community. I searched for some group or organization that was helping the people in Payatas. Eventually, through information from Catholic Relief Services, I came across the Mother Ignacia National Social Apostolate Center (MINSAC), part of the Congregation of the Religious of the Virgin Mary. Their work, in turn, was being supported by Catholic Charities of Edmonton in Alberta, Canada.

At one time I had been a pastor in one of our inner-city parishes. But I learned from the late Msgr. Bill Irwin, the longtime director of Catholic Charities in Edmonton, that the poverty in Payatas was beyond one's comprehension. The people there didn't even have something as basic as water. The water that was brought in to them was expensive and not always clean. Men, women, and children were dying because of the contaminated water, and families were forced to spend a significant portion of the little money they had to buy it.

So working with Catholic Charities in Edmonton, our parish and several neighboring ones launched a fund-raising campaign. We were able to raise $40,000. The money went to support a local cooperative for a water truck project. The project was important because it meant that the water would be less expensive. It would also be guaranteed to be clean, since the work of the cooperative was being overseen by MINSAC/Catholic Charities. In addition, it would allow those involved to become more self-sufficient. We were able to purchase two water trucks, which would serve about fifteen hundred families. I have never been to the Philippines, but Marc Barylo, the vice president of development for Catholic Charities in Edmonton, had been making yearly visits to Quezon City. When he returned from Payatas, he told me how well the project was working.

Despite our success, my heart still ached, knowing that there were so many people living in such wretched conditions and still many without a basic necessity such as clean water. In this day and age, no one should have to live like this. I certainly gained a deeper understanding of those words of Jesus that as a priest I had proclaimed in church and preached about: "I was thirsty and you gave me a drink" (Matthew 25:35); and "Anyone who gives you a cup of water to drink because you belong to Christ, amen, I say to you, will surely not lose his reward" (Mark 9:41).

Songs from the Promised Land

God had moved my heart to help the people of Payatas. With his grace we had been able to respond. But what happened next still surprises me to this day. And it soon became clear why the Lord had assigned me to the parish in Clyde.

An elderly woman in my parish became very ill. Her daughter, Nancy Bryan, who had been living for years in California, came back to Clyde to care for her. The woman passed away, but Nancy stayed on in her mother's house, and she and her husband, John, turned one of the bedrooms into a recording studio. I soon discovered that they were two incredibly talented people—Nancy's songs were even featured on a Grammy-nominated album!

That November I gave them a cassette tape of some songs that I had written in the seminary. They surprised me at Christmas by recording one of my songs. I was in awe of how incredibly captivating they had been able to make the song. That gave me an idea: We could produce a CD of the songs, with all the proceeds going to help the Payatas Community in the Philippines.

On the CD, which we called *Songs from the Promised Land*, we used five of the songs that I had written, four songs by Nancy and John, and two from another very talented local artist and friend of mine, Glenn McClure. It was a bittersweet moment for me, because the CD was completed just before my brother's death and a short time before my mother moved into a nursing home.

We have been able to raise $150,000 from the CD through donations for the people of Payatas. This incredible amount of money to help these "least of my brothers and sisters" showed me God's reason for my assignment to the Clyde/Savannah parish.

But I also realized that this project wasn't only about raising needed funds. It was also helping to raise awareness of the plight of people living in such heartbreaking conditions, especially in a predominantly Catholic nation. The CD has been sent to thirty-three states and nineteen countries, as well as to Philippine President Gloria Macapagal-Arroyo, the actor Martin Sheen (who has also helped out in Payatas), and Pope Benedict XVI, to name a few.

A Labor of Love

Songs for the Promised Land also gave me an appreciation of the parable of the talents (Matthew 25:14-30). These songs were just ordinary, but John and Nancy's labor of love made them outstanding. They spent one hundred hours alone in their recording studio on just one of the songs that I wrote ("Child of God"), and it shows! It made me think how God must feel when he sees us take one of the talents he has given us and turn it into something magnificent.

The people in Payatas live in such extreme conditions, yet as Msgr. Irwin once noted, they have such strong faith. As Jesus said, with faith we can move mountains. I believe, with Msgr. Irwin and Marc Barylo, that together we can transform this mountain of garbage into a monument of hope. I pray for this to happen every day. In fact, there have been many improvements in the living conditions in Payatas over the last ten years.

Over my thirty-five years as a priest, I have served alongside some wonderful staff and parishioners. Although I am not directly working with MINSAC, I am in awe of the strong faith and generous love of these women, who not only minister there but live day after day with the people in these incredible conditions. Even in these difficult circumstances, you can see in their faces a deep joy and an amazing hope. I feel privileged to be able to support them in a small way, and I hope that we are able to continue to help them in their many programs to lift the people of the Payatas Community out of such abject poverty.

As priests, we are conscious of so many difficulties, affecting not only our parishioners but also our brothers and sisters throughout our world. The danger for anyone facing such large problems is to feel overwhelmed and become paralyzed. Sometimes we priests can feel like we never do enough, but this whole endeavor has been a reminder to me of God's grace, working in ways that I could never have imagined. It is also a constant reminder to me of Jesus' words to the woman whose simple gesture of anointing him is remembered in the Scriptures (Mark 14:3-9): "She has done a good thing for me. . . . She has done what she could" (14:6, 8).

Fr. Hewes was born in East Rochester, New York, and was ordained in the Diocese of Rochester in 1974. He has served as director of Project Rachel for the diocese for the last thirteen years, and currently serves as parochial administrator of St. Joseph's Church in Rush, New York.

Chapter 22

Many Roads Lead to Brooklyn

Fr. Vincentius Toan Do

God has his eyes on those he calls, even before they are born. And if we trust in him, no obstacle, no difficulty, no detour can keep us from the journey he has planned for us—even if we have to travel the world to get there!

My story begins in Vietnam. Early in the 1970s, my parents responded to an appeal by the Archbishop of Hue, Vietnam, the Most Rev. Philip-Mary Dien Nguyen, to become missionaries. They and their firstborn daughter left the home they had just built to come to Saigon City and actively participate in the works of the Vietnamese Missionary Society. They were the first Vietnamese missionary family.

It was in the heart of that mission, when the Vietnam War was at its fiercest, that I was born, on Palm Sunday at three o'clock in the morning. After my birth, my family's landlord refused to let us back into the house because he superstitiously believed that I, the newborn infant, would bring him bad luck. As a result, I had to live my first two weeks of life in the sacristy of the mission's church.

On May 3 of the same year, on the feast of the apostles Philip and James, I was baptized at the mission center of the Vietnamese Missionary Society. Two foreign priests, an Italian and a Taiwanese, both missionaries in Vietnam, were present, as well as a seminarian of the Society, who agreed to be my godfather. Archbishop Nguyen was also happy to be my spiritual grandfather, and encouraged my parents to give me the name of St. Philip, his patron saint. Thus I was baptized Philip Toan Do.

After the war ended and the Communists took control of all Vietnam, the Vietnamese Missionary Society was disbanded and foreign priests were expelled. My family returned to ordinary life in a small village in the countryside of South Vietnam. Yet our lives were anything but ordinary. Groundlessly suspecting that my father was an intelligence agent, the Communist cadres constantly checked in on us. They often knocked on our doors at midnight and even killed our dogs.

The Odyssey to Freedom

Early in the 1980s, once again my family left our beloved house and began a different life. This time my father brought the family to a place near the sea, where it was easier to leave the country. There we began an odyssey to freedom that lasted an entire decade. We experienced everything from hunger and poverty to deception, betrayal, and imprisonment. We eventually had to separate. Half of the family remained with my father in Vietnam while the rest left and went to the United States.

Suddenly my father was a single parent. Concerned about the proper upbringing of his children, he decided to send us to his parents in the countryside. Under the guidance of my devout grandmother, I studied the catechism and received my first Communion. On Pentecost Sunday, when I was twelve, I was confirmed. From then on I became quite active in my parish. While studying English with the Salesian Brothers, I became intrigued by the brothers' simple lifestyle and began discerning a vocation to the consecrated life.

When I was sixteen, we were finally able to rejoin my mother in the U.S. A defining moment occurred that June morning when I was about to leave. While saying good-bye my grandmother repeatedly told me never to lose my faith, no matter where I went. Wishing to give her some assurance, I told her that once I arrived in the United States, I would pursue a vocation to the priesthood. As soon as the words escaped my mouth, I was dumbfounded. It was the first time I had ever said such a thing to anyone.

Together with my father and my siblings, I flew to Rochester in upstate New York. The rest of my family joyfully welcomed us at the airport. After almost ten years of separation, my family was once again united! O, what pen can describe the happiness! Ready to begin our new life, my family registered at the parish of St. Charles Borromeo in Greece, a suburb of Rochester.

Completely forgetting about the assurance I had given to my grandmother on the day that I left Vietnam, I enjoyed every bit of life at the Greece Olympia High School. Besides doing quite well academically, I was involved in many extracurricular activities and was even inducted into the National Honor Society and Greece's Youth Hall of Fame.

Yet God would not let me forget my last words to my grandmother. One spring day my father went to California to attend the wedding of my uncle. There he met my godfather, whom I had never known, and asked him to help me fulfill my promise to my grandmother. My godfather happened to be a friend of the vocation director of the Congregation of St. John the Baptist, a Chinese missionary order. After returning from the wedding, my father gave me the priest's contact information.

I began to correspond with the vocation director through mail and telephone. In the summer of that year, the priest asked me to "come and see." So two years after my arrival to the United States, at the age of eighteen, I embarked on the next major journey of my life. Accompanied by my father, I boarded a Greyhound bus and traveled across the country to Los Angeles to join the Congregation.

Yet it would still be a long road ahead to the priesthood. At the Congregation I graduated from high school and was sent to Taiwan to study Chinese. There I entered the novitiate and was given the religious name Vincentius. When my visa expired, I was sent to New York City for philosophy and Asian studies at Queens College. After making my first vows, I became very active in the Chinese and Vietnamese communities in Queens, running a very successful youth ministry. From there I was sent to Mount Angel Seminary in Oregon, where I received my bachelor's degree in philosophy, and then on to Rome for my theological studies.

At this point, however, I hit another bump in the road. I was weary of all the changes, and I discerned that God was calling me to a more stable life. I left Rome and returned to my family. After much prayer and discernment, I eventually left the Congregation and joined the Diocese of Brooklyn in New York. On the feast of the Immaculate Conception, December 8, 2006, I was ordained a deacon, and on June 2, 2007, I was ordained a priest by the Bishop of Brooklyn. I am now joyfully serving God's people as a parochial vicar at St. Rosalia-Regina Pacis Parish in Brooklyn, New York.

There are many roads that lead to Brooklyn, New York. I certainly didn't take the shortest route. But because it was his plan for me, the Lord made sure that I got there!

Fr. Vincentius Toan Do is a parochial vicar at St. Rosalia-Regina Pacis Parish in the Diocese of Brooklyn.

Chapter 23

Continuing the Healing Ministry of Jesus

Fr. Stefan P. Starzynski

S omeone once wrote that if you look at the public ministry of Jesus, you'll find that he is either leaving a healing or going to a healing. In fact, Jesus spent more time healing than preaching, and he healed people so that they would be open to his preaching. As I have come to know Jesus in a deeper, more intimate way through the thirteen years of my priesthood, I have felt him prompting me to continue his healing ministry in our own day.

When I first entered the seminary, I didn't connect faith with a personal relationship with the Lord. I went to Mass and prayed the Rosary every day, and I loved to study theology and apologetics. If you had asked me, "Is Jesus the center of your life?" I would have answered, "Yes, he must be, because I am in the seminary." However, looking back, I am not sure that he was. I am not sure that I knew the person of Jesus.

A turning point in my life came when my spiritual director at the seminary encouraged me to read the Bible each day. I was not a Bible reader, but I did begin this practice at his suggestion. I found that immersing myself in Scripture helped my faith to become more rooted in a personal, intimate relationship with Jesus.

I remember being in my room in the seminary a couple of weeks before my ordination. I asked the Lord, "Do you want me to become a priest?" I took the Bible off my shelf and opened it at random. I opened it up to the beginning of the Acts of the Apostles, where Jesus says to the apostles, "Wait here, and in a little while, you will receive power from on high when the Holy Spirit comes upon you, and you will be my witnesses in Jerusalem, Judea, Samaria, and to the ends of the earth" (see Acts 1:8). When I read these words, I knew that Jesus was speaking to me directly through his word, and that yes, he wanted me to "wait here" and become a priest.

Receiving the Holy Spirit

Two weeks later, on May 18, 1996, I was ordained. Someone told me that whatever I prayed for, I would receive, so I said to Jesus as I was lying face down on the floor, "Jesus, I know that I will be a priest in a sacramental sense, but I want to be baptized in the Holy Spirit in the Pentecostal sense also." Two days after my ordination, on May 20, 1996, I was at a prayer service at a local parish, and I was baptized in the Holy Spirit.

On my ordination day, my friend Mary Beth said that her neighbor's baby was very ill, and months after his birth, he was still in the hospital. She asked if I would pray with him. I left my party and went to the hospital. I remember seeing tubes all over the place. I asked the parents, "Do you believe that if I anoint your baby, he will be healed?" They said yes, and I anointed him. Three days later I got a call that the baby had been miraculously healed. I think it is symbolic that the first sacrament that I celebrated was the anointing of a sick baby and that he was healed. Since that day, praying for healing is an important part of my ministry.

After I was assigned to my first parish, I asked the pastor if I could hold Mass and healing services. He had just one question: Would I have enough energy to do my parish work and these healing services? I prayed about it, and I came to the Book of Daniel. After Daniel is captured, the king orders him to be given a portion of the royal ration of food and wine, but Daniel does not want to eat foods that are prohibited by the law. So he makes a deal with the palace guards: He will eat only vegetables and water for ten days, and then they can see if he looks weak in comparison to the other men who are eating the royal foods. Daniel not only does not look weaker in comparison, but he looks stronger (see Daniel 1:1-16). The meaning of the Scripture for me was that in doing the Mass and healing services, I would have more energy, not less. While it is true that after some Masses, I am totally exhausted, the overall effect is that I have more energy.

I celebrate a Mass and healing service once a month. I have learned that there is no right or wrong way to pray for healing. God has given each person his or her own style. We can learn from others, but we are not to copy them exactly. In fact, our own way of praying for healing can and does change over time, and even from person to person. The minute we think we have our own method, God changes it. The most important ingredient is faith: the faith of the person doing the praying or the person being prayed over. But even that is not an absolute. There have been people who claim to have no faith or little faith who have been healed.

Holding these prayer services is a valuable part of my priesthood. Sometimes I feel like an odd duck—I am one of the only priests in my diocese that conducts healing services. I think many priests feel uncomfortable praying for people, but I think it ought to be part of every priest's life. I have had the blessing of seeing many miracles.

It is a blessing to see the fruit of prayer. We often think that faith means believing without seeing. Maybe it's because I am weak, but it helps my faith to see prayers for healing being answered and miracles happening. I rejoice when I see God moving among his people!

Fr. Stefan Starzynski was born in Bangkok, Thailand, in 1969 and grew up in Arlington, Virginia. He was ordained a priest for the Diocese of Arlington on May 18, 1996, and has served in several parishes in the diocese. He is currently the parochial vicar at St Mary of Sorrows in Fairfax, Virginia. He is also the author of Miracles: Healing in a Broken World.

Chapter 24

In Praise of Horizontal Prayer

Fr. Frank Moan, SJ

I'm seventy-seven and retired, a priest, a celibate. You may be like me. Or you may be married still, with or without your spouse. You may be a parent, a grandparent, or, God bless you, a great-grandparent. Or you may be single, young, with the expectation of many years ahead. In any event, I hope each of you shares with me the joy of horizontal prayer.

By horizontal prayer I mean, literally, horizontal: when I'm on my back, in bed. Age has taught me that I do some of my best praying in bed. I still advocate that parents teach their children to kneel at bedside in the evening to say their prayers. But my knees will no longer let me get down there. And if I do get down, I would have to call out to someone else in the rectory to get me up. God understands. In fact, I think God can't wait till I get flat on my back in bed.

I do my best praying then. Sometimes, if I've had a very long and stressful day, I might fall asleep almost immediately. But that is rare. Generally, I have to lie there for a while before sleep comes. That's when I pray.

I converse with God about the day I've spent, how it went, where I failed God or my neighbor, what graces came my way and how well I used them. I like to talk to God about the people

I encountered that day, in person, on the phone, through e-mail or snail mail. I often tell God how I disagree with the way he is letting world turn round. I pray for those who die each day in Iraq or Afghanistan. I pray for understanding among Muslims, Christians, and Jews.

I also turn often to Mary, the Mother of Jesus. I say at least one Hail Mary to win Our Lady's protection. My life in the liturgical practices of the Church has taught me that the day never ends without recourse to Our Lady.

Prayer to Mary then turns my mind to the communion of saints. Over many years, I have come to love and respect so many of them that I count them as intimate friends on whom I can depend to be voices for me before the Trinity. And in that number I include many people I have known over these past seventy-seven years who have preceded me to the pearly gates.

At my age—those who are about my age will know what I'm talking about—I have to get up periodically to relieve my bladder. I take a nightly pill to forestall such an occurrence. But it never does. I think I take the pill just to keep my doctor happy. Anyway, I get up at least twice a night and return to bed. Now, sometimes I am lucky and soon fall back to sleep. But often it is not so easy.

So here I am again, turning to prayer. I begin to think about the next day. And the first thing I think is: Will I have a next day? Or will God summon me before then? It is not a pessimistic thought. Many of my relatives and friends have died before this age. The daily obituary notices recount many deaths of people my age, older, and younger. So I'm wont to say that prayer I learned in childhood. It may be childish, but it is a beautiful prayer and means a great deal to me at this age: "Now I lay me down to sleep; I pray the Lord my soul to keep. If I should die before I wake, I pray the Lord my soul to take." I have known some of my fellow Jesuits who have died peacefully in their sleep or while sitting in their chair. I envy them—it's a nice way to go.

Then I turn to the coming day, if God should grant it. I recall the intention for the Mass I will celebrate. It may be for a deceased brother Jesuit, or for a relative with cancer, or for our country in this time of national crisis. I talk to God about that intention. I bring God up-to-date on where I am politically, charitably, socially. I must admit I do much of the talking. But sometimes God does get through. I begin to see things more clearly. I realize there were times I was hasty in judgment or insensitive in action. I see new ideas opening up before me on how I can contribute to the graces God spreads through his Church, particularly through its sacramental life.

I give some thought also to the Divine Office, the Breviary I shall be reading when I get up. It will take some time over the course of the day. Nowadays I pray it with much more devotion than I did in my earlier years. I give extra attention to it because I now read it on behalf of all the priests in my diocese. I know many of them are too busy to read it, so I read it for them.

The middle of the night gives me the time to raise to God the many friends I have from over seventy years, particularly those who are now in physical distress. A ninety-two-year-old friend prays daily that she may die. I ask, God, why don't you let her die? She would be so much happier with you than she is now, with a body that refuses to respond to her willingness to love others.

I pray for my friend the doctor who, shortly after retiring, suffered a debilitating stroke. Since then he has lost a leg and, worse still, lost much of his enthusiasm for life. I pray for his wife, a nurse with physical problems of her own that prevent her from giving her husband the full attention he needs. Dear God, you know what wonderful people these have been, how much they have done for others in very active lives. Yet now they wait. God, give them patience; give them cheer.

I pray for a widow friend of forty years' acquaintance. Not only has she lost her husband; she also has buried two of her five children. Yes, she has the others to look after her. But God, she is failing. Give her courage; give her comfort. And give her children the willingness to look after her, without depriving their own children of the attention they deserve.

I could stay up all night praying for these and myriad other causes.

On a rare occasion nowadays, I am awakened by the alarm to rise and go to a nearby parish to say early Mass. That breaks my momentum of prayer.

Ordinarily, I can get up when I wake up. Or I can lie there for a few or many minutes. I can pray again. Today, dear God, this day is for you. You have given me another day to live, or maybe only part of the day. If you call me home today, I hope I shall be rejoicing to greet you. But if I am to live another day, may it be to your glory. Let me bring sunshine into someone else's life; let me be a support to my fellow Jesuits here in the rectory; let me learn how to converse with you, dear God, more and more. Teach me to pray.

I open my eyes. I look to see if the sun is shining on the church-school building outside my window. How I am cheered if it does. I see in my room all the souvenirs of a long life. They speak to me of so many past and present loves. They are my daily comforts. Each speaks a prayer to me; I speak a prayer to each.

Then it is time to rise. As I put my feet into my slippers, I offer a final prayer. God, I'm going about the day. I may not be as attentive to you throughout this day as I have been during this night. So please remember that I love you still. I'm here to do your will. And should you bring me to another night, I'll lie again in bed, and our conversation will go on. ⌇

Fr. Frank Moan, SJ, is a native of Baltimore and served as chaplain of Georgetown University Law School before becoming coordinator of the American branch of the Jesuit Refugee Service. He resides at the St. Claude La Colombiére Jesuit Community in Baltimore, Maryland. This article originally appeared in America *magazine.*

Chapter 25

I Believe in Miracles

Fr. John Adams

My ministry as a priest and my ministry to the poor go hand in hand. And what I have witnessed over the years has reaffirmed my belief in the miracle of God's presence in our world residing within the human heart. I believe in miracles—miracles of divine providence and miracles of people who were beaten down by life but turned their lives around with the help of their brothers and sisters.

Growing up in Erie, Pennsylvania, in a close-knit family, the second of seven children, I learned firsthand about sharing and the goodness of people. Both my parents were loving, kind, and generous to us, and taught us to be that way with others. My father, a hardworking man with a good job in a steel-related factory, was severely injured when I was nine years old. He lost his job, never recovered his health, and for years could do only menial odd jobs. We barely survived.

However, it was the dignified, quiet help of the nuns in the parish, who gave us food and clothing, that enabled us to survive. We couldn't afford the tuition for Catholic school, but the pastor, with dignified charity, persuaded Mom and made it possible for us to attend. Inspired by the example of kindness and faith of those sisters, priests, and my parents, I entered a high school seminary at the age of fourteen. The seminary was training us to become foreign missionaries, bringing the word of God to the far corners of the world.

By the time I was in my second year of college, however, my dad's condition worsened. I decided to stay closer to home, so I joined the Claretian Fathers and Brothers, who serve here in the U.S. During my novitiate in 1963, our family experienced Dad's traumatic death. He was only in his midforties, and my youngest brother was only a baby. At the time I seriously contemplated leaving the seminary to help support my family. Again, divine providence stepped in. My mother insisted I return to the novitiate while the Claretian community insisted on helping my family quietly with a bit of monthly financial help. The community, in their words, was "dedicated to seeing the world through the eyes of the poor and responding to their most urgent and timely needs." Their formation was pivotal to my vocation.

The Poor and Homeless as Christ

The Claretians sent me to Catholic University to study philosophy and theology, and then for graduate education in social work, which gave me the tools to implement my faith in real and concrete ways. I was ordained to the priesthood in 1969, and my first assignment was in Chicago as a psychiatric social worker. But through prayer and discernment, I felt called to reach out to the very poor.

In 1973 I began working in Alexandria, Virginia, with others who wanted to live out the gospel and serve the poor in a real way. We began Christ House under the auspices of Catholic Charities to serve meals to the poor, and provide clothing and shelter to families and single adults. Though I knew Christ in daily prayer and the Mass, Christ House was a wonderful beginning of really getting to know the poor and homeless as Christ because we shared our meals with our guests daily. And, in doing so, I can truly say that our eyes were opened! Christ became very real to me.

In 1978 Fr. Horace McKenna, SJ, invited me to come to Washington, D. C., to help with So Others Might Eat (SOME), a fledgling soup kitchen on North Capitol Street, which is in sight of the U.S. Capitol dome. Fr. McKenna had started SOME eight years earlier with the support of Msgr. Ralph Kuehner, Baptist minister Rev. Griffin Smith, and several laypersons.

When I came to SOME, we were serving two meals a day, seven days a week, for about sixty people but offered no other services. SOME did not even have a working stove, and soup had to be prepared on a neighbor's stove. It was really "garbage soup" made from food collected from dumpsters, which I thought was not what we should be serving our brothers and sisters. But from the very beginning, we experienced God's providence. The Sisters of Mercy gave us a grant to buy a new stove so that we could cook. We began to look for volunteer churches to help us provide decent, hot, nutritious food daily.

At that time I had concluded that it was everyone's faith that calls us to take care of the poor, and this was my first wonderful interfaith experience of working not only with our Catholic parishes but also with synagogues and Protestant churches. In a very short while, we had over one hundred faith groups committed to bringing a casserole meal to serve once a month. Our meal program grew to serving over one thousand meals a day.

We also added shower facilities, a clothing room, and with the help of the Georgetown University Dental School, a full dental clinic, followed by an all-volunteer medical clinic staffed with volunteer nurses and doctors. The dining room was renovated so that it would accommodate many more guests in a brightly colored, clean, welcoming environment. Our volunteers and staff not only serve our guests but also welcome them with a smile, a kind word, or a handshake. When visitors come to our SOME facilities, they are surprised at the atmosphere; I have often said that "we should serve the poor, but we should not do it poorly."

Providing direct services to the poor is vital, but from the beginning, we knew we had to address the root causes of poverty and homelessness for our guests. The main reasons why people are homeless are serious mental illness, unemployment, drug addiction, and/or lack of affordable housing. SOME has developed very successful professional programs that address all of these issues, and we continue to restore hope and dignity to literally thousands each year. Affordable housing for families and SROs (Single Room Occupancy) for transitional or permanent housing is now a major goal of our housing development initiative, working with private donors and government agencies. SOME currently provides 350 units of long-term, dignified, safe housing for individuals and families, including 150 children. Advocacy efforts and social justice education help to empower our clients and ensure their visibility before the government and private organizations.

Sustained on the Journey

Many have asked what sustains me in this journey. What keeps me going? Above all, it is my faith and my prayer life. I have been a priest for forty years now and in the Archdiocese of Washington for over twenty-six years; Cardinal James Hickey welcomed me and was a strong supporter of our work with the poor at SOME. He visited and served meals here, but he also listened to the stories of the homeless people.

I have also been encouraged and supported in my journey by our wonderful, small faith community of women and men, the Community of Christ. We meet weekly to share our journeys together with prayer, a meal, Mass, and a commitment to not only serve the poor but to walk the journey with them. I have been enriched by each of them. Equally, my faith has been influenced by my friends and mentors, Fr. McKenna and Msgr. Kuehner, as well as several other faithful priest friends with whom I have been close since our days in the seminary. I am enriched in liturgy and prayer when I visit my home in Erie and stay with my Benedictine family; my youngest sister is Benedictine, and this community deepens both my faith journey and friendships.

In addition, I have been sustained by the many people who have come through SOME, people whom I have gotten to know so well. Their faith, their struggles, and their courage are truly inspiring. As I witness their lives transformed with the help of SOME's very dedicated, professional, and compassionate staff, I recall what the late Fr. McKenna called "slow miracles."

One woman, JoAnn, came to SOME to eat; she was homeless and addicted to drugs. She had lost her children to "the system" and was beaten down. She was overcome by the hospitality she received and lack of condescension. She slowly began to trust again, and then entered our inpatient drug treatment program, based on the very spiritual AA program, followed by our job training, which she finished. She found a job, had her children restored, married, bought a townhouse—and now works at SOME! She is truly a woman of courage and faith who inspires me.

One of the great things about being at SOME for over thirty-one years is that I see many "JoAnns" who have gone through our programs and are supporting themselves and their families, and giving back by volunteering. Over twenty percent of our staff are formerly homeless, and two former homeless persons are on our board of directors.

I have deepened my journey through witnessing God at work in the many staff and volunteers who live out the gospel message of Matthew 25: "Whatever you do for one of my sisters or brothers, you do for me." SOME is privileged to have enormously dedicated laypersons who have dedicated themselves to the poor. Richard Gerlach, who came to SOME with me thirty-one years ago, is now executive director. During this time, he married, and now his children volunteer at SOME.

I have learned more and more to be thankful and to trust in God's providence through our terrific volunteers who provide their services as doctors, nurses, cooks, tutors, and attorneys; through the people of means, who are major donors wanting to make a difference; and through our dedicated board of directors, who all want to share in walking the journey with the poor and in making a difference through their donations of time and talent. SOME would not exist without them or without our donors on whom we depend. SOME is blessed by each and every one. All, poor and rich, are witnesses to those "slow miracles" of restoring hope and dignity to our homeless brothers and sisters.

Fr. John Adams has directed So Others May Eat *for the past thirty years. For more information about SOME, or if you'd like to support SOME's ministry, go to www.some.org. SOME has just published* Slow Miracles *in honor of its fortieth anniversary, which can be ordered online at its Web site.*

Chapter 26

Celibacy: A Sign of Love for Jesus

The Most Rev. Victor Galeone
Bishop of St. Augustine

Bishop Galeone delivered this homily to the priests in his diocese at the Chrism Mass on March 27, 2002, just after the pedophilia scandal involving priests hit the news media.

I'd like you to come back with me to the spring of 1974—back to the town of Andahuaylas, high in the Andes Mountains. At the time I was serving as a missionary in Peru. This particular Sunday afternoon, I was visiting our sick parishioners in the town hospital. In the men's ward, I came across Oswaldo—a Lutheran minister who was visiting from Lima. He had taken ill a few days before. At this point I'd like to quote directly from a journal that I sometimes keep:

On the night table next to Oswaldo's bed was a pocket-sized New Testament. "May I?" I asked as I picked it up. Thumbing through the small volume, I noticed that he had underlined some pertinent verses, but only a few. It was then that I saw it. Verse 12 of Matthew 19 was very deliberately underlined: ". . . and there are eunuchs who have made themselves so for the sake of the kingdom of Heaven. Let the one who can accept this teaching do so."

Setting the small volume down, I inquired, "Oswaldo, may I ask how old you are?" "Twenty-four," he replied. "Are you married?" I asked. "No, I'm not." I smiled knowingly. "Why are you smiling?" he asked. "I think that I've just discovered a beautiful secret." Now he was the one who smiled, and he looked away as he remarked, "Yes, Victor, for as long as the Lord gives me the grace to do so. And I pray that it will be to my dying breath."

In my journal I concluded with this observation: "Lord, what a sad contrast! So many of my brother priests becoming bitter over this 'burden, forced on them by an outdated, medieval Church'— and here we have a separated brother, unassumingly and joyfully accepting this beautiful gift from your hands."

My brothers in the Lord, in these days when fresh allegations of clergy misconduct are surfacing almost daily, when the media seems intent on painting the priesthood in the worst possible light, when we priests find ourselves under a dark cloud of suspicion, it is essential that we never lose sight of the One we are serving and why we are serving him.

Most of us can relate to the idealism of young Oswaldo, because years ago the Lord looked out and fixed his eyes on us as well. Whether we were still in our youth, or middle-aged, or close to our senior years, Jesus looked at each one of us here and said, "My son, give me your heart!"

In those heady days of our first calling, we replied with self-assured confidence: "Lord, my heart is yours. You alone are worthy of all my love."

If our sacrifice entailed one generous outpouring of blood as in the case of the early martyrs, most of us would rise to the challenge. Instead, the Lord is asking us to endure a dry martyrdom: to repeat with him, day after day, especially in troubling moments of temptation, "Lord, this is my body, now given for you! This is my life, poured out for all . . ."

Puzzled, the skeptic asks: *"Why this lifelong fast from one of nature's noblest drives? Why such a waste? And for what purpose?"*

I quote the answer that the French philosopher, Jean Guitton, gave years ago: "In an age so steeped in sex and pleasure-seeking materialism, should there not be somewhere on this planet those who joyously and generously offer their bodies as concrete proof of their conviction of the supremacy of the spiritual over the material, and as a sign of their love for him who did not spare even his own Son for love of us?"

Amused, the skeptic continues: *"But doesn't your vow debase the elevated state of marriage?"*

Far from demeaning marriage, the Church considers the love embrace between husband and wife as God's most precious gift to us on the natural level. So precious, indeed, that she insists that her priests, brothers, and sisters offer it to God as the finest natural gift that we possess—much like an engagement ring that's given to the beloved. After all, isn't God worthy of the very best?

"Ah," retorts the skeptic. *"Fine sounding words to conceal what, at root, is an aberration!"*

David Hartman, a minister of the Church of the Nazarene and himself married, made this comment some ten years ago:

"Of course celibacy is an aberration—an aberration because of the normal human drive to mate and procreate. It is, in its own way, as much of an aberration as a soldier throwing himself on a grenade to save the life of his buddies, or God dying on a cross.

"In other words," Hartman continued, "celibates who are celibate for the sake of the kingdom are engaged in a lifelong act of self-denial. One might even say that those who are celibate for the sake of their priestly vocation are heroic; for is there not something heroic in one who surrenders his life in such an extraordinary way for such invisible, transcendent ends?"

"But what of all the failures?" objects the skeptic. *"Aren't they a counterwitness?"*

Sad to say, they are. They only prove what St. Paul said to the Ephesians: "Our struggle is not with flesh and blood, but with the powers of darkness and with the spiritual forces of evil" (see 6:12).

Yes, we're engaged in real warfare! And real warfare produces real casualties. But let's take heart in King David and Simon Peter. Repentant, they returned to serve the Lord as wounded healers— more committed than ever.

This year, in his letter to priests, our Holy Father expressed his profound sorrow over the betrayal of the grace of ordination by some of our brothers. Then he goes on to say, and I quote: "All of us—conscious of our human weakness, but trusting in the healing power of divine grace—are called to embrace the mystery of the Cross and to commit ourselves more fully to the search for holiness" (*Letter to Priests for Holy Thursday 2002*, 11).

Brothers, in a few moments we'll all be standing to renew our commitment to the Lord as we repeat the vow we made years ago. As we do so, let's "commit ourselves more fully to the search for holiness" that John Paul speaks of. Specifically, let's renew our commitment to:

- Daily prayer, especially the time we spend in the presence of our Eucharistic Lord.
- Regular confession to the same brother priest, at least on a monthly basis.
- The Rosary. The old saying is so true: "Behind every successful man there stands a woman." Jesus gave us his mother to be that woman in our lives.
- The support of our peers. Our prime companionship should be with our priest friends.
- Regular exercise. Some form of strenuous exertion is essential to maintaining our physical and emotional balance.
- Monitoring our entertainment. Much of what's on TV and the Internet is not conducive to leading a chaste life. Even worse, it can become an addiction.

My brothers, I close with this final thought: If we are truly serious about reflecting the image of Jesus in our lives, we'll experience the truth of what we heard in the first reading:

You will be called priests of the LORD,
  you will be named ministers of our God. . . .
All who see you will acknowledge you,

as a race that the LORD has blessed.
(see Isaiah 61:6, 9)

Bishop Victor Galeone was born in Philadelphia in 1935 and raised in Baltimore. He was ordained in Rome on December 18, 1960. On his return to Baltimore, he served as parochial vicar, pastor, professor, and principal of the day seminary, as well as a missionary in Peru for eleven years. On August 21, 2001, he was ordained the ninth bishop of the Diocese of St. Augustine in Florida.

Chapter 27

The Grass Is Green Everywhere

Fr. James Martin, SJ

An older Jesuit once told me he felt that priests have a much harder life than laypeople. We're always "on call," he explained, and have so many responsibilities—celebrating Masses, hearing confessions, living in community, preparing homilies, and the like. Laypeople can set their own schedules, he said. Therefore, he concluded, priests need much more vacation time than laypeople—perhaps two months a year would be adequate.

At the time, I had the presence of mind to tell my friend that he was out of his.

On the other hand, a surprising number of people have told me (particularly since my ordination) how jealous they are of my life, not because of any sort of spiritual satisfaction, but because it must be so . . . "relaxing," as someone put it. It must be great, one parishioner commented, to have everything you need! You never have any worries, and what's more, the Church will always take care of you. It must be nice, she said, in a manner that telegraphed her distinct disapproval for such a cosseted life. Even though this happened after Mass at the parish "coffee hour," and I was surrounded by other parishioners, I was able quietly to remind her of such things as the occasional loneliness of the celibate, the always imperfect dynamics of religious communities, and the fact that I was, in point of fact, working on a Sunday.

All of this came to mind over the Christmas holidays, after spending some time at home with my sister and brother-in-law.

Almost two years ago, my sister gave birth to a boy, named Charles, who almost instantly became the center of our family, or at least its joyful heart. Now, I had of course heard that grandparents go "ga-ga," as one says, over their grandchildren, but it was quite another thing to see my father down on all fours in the living room with a year-old toddler, and my mother's face light up whenever she heard a high-pitched voice shout, "Nanny!" Even more surprising was the instantaneous and intense love I felt for my little nephew. Taking the train back to New York after Christmas, I realized that just a few hours after leaving home, I already missed him. Missing someone whose total vocabulary consists of fifty words! (Believe it or not, "dot-com" is one of them, which may give you an idea of how many Christmas gifts his parents bought online.)

But, as any sentient human being knows, babies and toddlers and children require a breathtaking amount of attention. Shortly after my nephew's birth, I spent a night at my sister's house, sleeping (or rather trying to sleep) in the room next to the baby, who woke up four times that night. The next morning I was completely wiped out—and I wasn't the one who had to feed him! Until I witnessed my sister and brother-in-law in action, I literally could not have imagined the amount of time and effort babies demand and how dead tired parents could get.

So when the baby woke for the third time, I suddenly remembered my Jesuit friend and his comment about a layperson's life being easy. And I thought: I doubt that he will ever have to wake up four times a night regularly. (On the other hand, my sister and brother-in-law won't be celebrating three Masses in a row any time soon.)

But better to consider it this way: Each person's life has a full measure of joys and struggles, meaningful to that person. I look at my sister with some envy, but also wonder how anyone can raise a child and not be consumed with worry. (If I love and worry about my nephew, how much more must his parents?) And while religious life is often a challenge, it's enormously satisfying to follow one's vocation, whether you're single or married or ordained or living the vowed life.

And so, I think, it's good to spend time on both sides of the fence. It helps one to realize that, in the end, the grass is wonderfully green everywhere.

Fr. James Martin, SJ, is the associate editor of America *magazine and the author of several best-selling books, including* My Life with the Saints. *This article originally appeared in* America *magazine.*

Chapter 28

Sharing a Meal and a Common Vocation

Fr. Frank Lechiara

I have been a priest for fifty years. When I look back over that time, as well as the years before when I was discerning the call to the priesthood and studying in the seminary, I am grateful for the support and encouragement I have received. And I am especially grateful to my brother priests from the neighboring parishes where I have served. Each week we have gathered together to share a meal, and each week I thank the Lord for the priesthood that we share.

I first felt a great desire to become a priest when I was in the ninth grade. I was attending a religion class for students who were in the public school system. At that time there was an early-release program that allowed students in the public schools to attend religion class each week in a denomination of their choice. During this particular class, Sr. Marietta asked if anyone had ever thought about becoming a priest or entering religious life. Several of us raised our hands, and she asked us to see her after class. Then she gave me a card from the diocesan vocation office and asked me to fill it out.

Several weeks later, a priest from the vocation office came to visit my parents and me. He explained the process of entering the seminary and what would be expected of those who would be accepted. I was a good student in school, and I was sure that I would have no trouble with the studies required in the seminary. After he had left, my parents expressed their joy that I wanted to become a priest, but my father was concerned that I was still immature and felt that I should finish high school and then consider entering the seminary. I was heartbroken. I replied that if I didn't enter now, I would probably never enter. My father very calmly explained that if God was calling me, the call would still be there when I finished high school.

Although I was disappointed, I was resigned to the fact that I would have to wait. I lived the life of an ordinary high school student. I was involved in school activities, I kept up my grades, and occasionally I thought about the seminary. Then a good friend of mine, who attended the parish school, invited me to come to a Sodality meeting on a Sunday evening. I was happy to attend. However, he had to get permission from the religious sister in charge, since the Sodality membership was for the parish high school students only. Lucky for me, the sister was happy to let me join. After the meetings, we would attend Sunday night Benediction.

After graduation I got a job working in the office of an oil well supply company. I continued to attend Benediction services on Sundays. One Sunday night I was at Benediction, and when the priest blessed us with the Blessed Sacrament, I felt a calm come over me. When I came home, I told my parents that I had come to the conclusion that God was calling me to become a priest. They were delighted and told me to continue praying.

Before entering the seminary, however, I needed to learn Latin. So I asked Sr. Marietta if she would teach me. She was delighted.

Each night during the week, I left work and stopped at the convent for my lessons. After several months I applied for entrance to the seminary and was accepted. A whole new world opened up for me. My family and friends were very supportive, and I found that the college seminary was a great challenge.

Throughout my days in the seminary, I often thought about my first inkling of a calling and all the things that had transpired during those years. I couldn't believe that God would call me! I knew of others who would have been great priests, and I marveled at the fact that all of this was happening to me. I enjoyed my studies a great deal. I would take notes in shorthand, and then transcribe them and sell them to some of my classmates. Before exams we would go over the notes and study together. It was a great moment of sharing, and the feeling of camaraderie was overwhelming.

Guess Who's Coming to Dinner?

At my first assignment as a priest, I was fortunate to be in an area where a kind pastor brought the priests in the area into his rectory. He was most hospitable and very helpful to those of us who were just starting out. When I was transferred, I remarked to this great priest that I would miss the camaraderie of the other priests. He told me that I should think about continuing this same custom where I would be stationed. At first I was a little reluctant to do anything. But after a few months, I realized how much these gatherings had helped me, and I knew I should continue them. So I would call my mother and ask her how to make different foods. Then I would prepare a dinner and invite neighboring priests to join us.

Each time I was transferred, I would start a new group. My cooking skills improved tremendously, and I looked forward to each of our gatherings. This sharing with my comrades would continue throughout my fifty years as a priest, and continues even now. In the parish in which I am now stationed, I am still blessed with the support of my fellow priests.

Each Sunday evening a group of us (anywhere from six to twelve priests) gets together for dinner and spends several hours sharing stories, ideas, aspirations, and hopes. I prepare the dinner and serve it. The rest help clean up and do the dishes. We also help each other out with Penance services, healing Masses, confessions for the schoolchildren, and parish missions. Now we are reviving the Forty Hours devotion in our diocese, and we continue to help one another. After each of our gatherings, I always reflect on how blessed I have been and how grateful I am to have been called by God to serve him in his priesthood.

Fr. Frank Lechiara was born in 1932 in Bradford, Pennsylvania, and was ordained on May 7, 1959, in Erie. After transferring to the Archdiocese of Miami in 1964, he earned a doctorate from the University of Miami and taught in the religion and education departments and also served as chaplain for the school's football team. He has served as principal of a diocesan high school as well as pastor at several parishes and as vicar of education of the diocese. Since 1992 he has been the pastor of St. Edward's Church in Palm Beach.

Chapter 29

My Long Journey to Africa

Fr. William A. Ryan

The year was 1938. A young Jesuit seminarian with a wrenching decision to make knelt alone in the chapel late at night in front of the tabernacle, the red sanctuary lamp flickering to the side, and prayed for discernment. Should he continue his formation for the priesthood, or was the Lord now calling him to turn in his cassock, leave the Society of Jesus, and embark on another path?

My father was reserved about his interior life and preferred not to speak about that spiritual struggle, but it surely was a difficult one. Just as surely, however, he was guided by the Holy Spirit to the right decision. As he prayed, he could not have known that of the eight children he would one day have, one son, myself, would become a diocesan priest, and another, my brother Peter, would enter the same novitiate he had attended and go on to be a Jesuit priest. But God did know, and held in the palm of his hand during those anguished moments not only my father and his sons, but also the thousands of Togolese who seventy years later are now entrusted to my pastoral care here in the African missions.

How did I come to be here? Only from the perspective of heaven will we fully understand how here on earth God uses persons and circumstances, events, and our own free choices to weave the wondrous pattern of our lives. But even now we can recognize certain key influences and connections, and at times we can see how he uses even crosses and evils to lead us along the path he has prepared for us. In this Year for Priests, I offer to him this story of my own vocation with praise and thanksgiving for his gift of the priesthood. I pray that my story might help, in some small way, those who read it to believe more deeply that everything God does is good, even when we cannot understand what he is up to, and to live out their own calling more faithfully.

Until shortly before entering the seminary, I rarely gave thought to the priesthood as a possible vocation. At the end of my senior year in 1972 at Georgetown University, I was unsure what to do with my life. Since Africa had always held a fascination for me, after graduation I decided to join the Peace Corps with the hope of seeing that great continent and perhaps doing some good while I was there. My application was accepted, and my departure for Togo was set for late January of the following year.

Drawn to the Pro-Life Movement

In the meantime I had become interested in the emerging pro-life movement. I spent much of those last few months before my departure distributing pro-life literature on several college campuses and doing "sidewalk counseling" with a couple of friends outside abortion clinics in the Washington area, offering help and alternatives to the sad, often frightened women as they arrived. One day when I told my father of our concern that the Church do more to defend unborn children, he said, "Why don't you talk to Cardinal [Patrick] O'Boyle about it? I know a priest who can get you an appointment."

So there we were, shortly before my departure date for Togo, sitting in the office of the Archbishop of Washington. As we nervously tried to tell him how we thought the parishes could be more involved in supporting pro-life efforts in the Maryland legislature, the Cardinal listened kindly. When we were finished, he asked us, with his slight Irish brogue, "Gentlemen, have you listened to the radio this morning?" We looked at each other and said we had not. "The Supreme Court has just legalized abortion throughout the land," he said. It was January 22, 1973, the day *Roe v. Wade* was decided. Pro-lifers came to regard that day as Black Monday, and in more ways than one, it was. When we walked out of the building, I thought I had never seen the sky darker or uglier, as torrents of rain poured down.

I considered canceling my Peace Corps plans in order to continue my pro-life work, but decided I ought to go. In less than a week, I was in Africa, where the seed of my missionary vocation, and in many ways of my priestly vocation itself, would be sown.

Peace Corps applicants cannot select their countries, but they can express a general preference. I had asked to go somewhere in sub-Saharan Africa, but to a place where I could get to Mass on Sunday. I hoped to keep at least that lifeline to God and to the faith while in Africa, but did not expect to experience much more of the Church than that. I was in for a surprise. After our in-country training, I was assigned to a small village whose lay catechist had worked there for many years. We became fast friends, and he was able to take me spiritually "behind the scenes," so to speak, and to show me the concrete and tangible impact of evangelization in the lives of the villagers. I slowly began to realize that those who seemed most fulfilled and happy, those who seemed to be living the noblest lives in spite of their severe poverty, were the practicing Catholics. Since these people had a cultural background so vastly different from my own, my eyes were opened to the meaning of "Catholic" as universal.

Under the Mango Tree

The Peace Corps has a rule against volunteers evangelizing, and I began to bend if not break that rule. I visited families, and as we chatted in front of their huts, I often encouraged them in their faith. Many evenings after supper, I sat under a mango tree in front of my house and prayed the Rosary, using beads my father gave me just before I left. When people saw I had put away my rosary, they would stop by to chat. Groups of children would come with their lanterns and sing songs, often Christian hymns they had learned. Years later during one of my visits to the village, one of the women pointed to that tree and said, "That's where God called you to be a priest, right there under that mango tree!"

I worked in a well-digging program, and traveled to villages on my Yamaha motorcycle to organize well projects and then supervise them. Our equipment was rudimentary, and since we often encountered rock we could not drill through, we had many failures. But we were able to complete a few wells during my two years. That was always a cause of great joy for villages that suffered from severe water problems.

In America we take clean water for granted, and it is hard for us to imagine what it is like to have to walk long distances for dirty water. Still, I began to observe that, important as it was, clean water by itself was not enough to ensure people's happiness or give meaning to their lives. Villagers who now had abundant potable water for the first time soon became used to it, and other problems continued or arose. Jesus himself needed natural water and asked for some from the Samaritan woman, but I began to reflect on what he then went on to tell her: Water from a well quenches thirst for a time, but he came to offer us living water that springs up to eternal life (see John 4:5-42).

Things began to fit together into a larger picture. God had called me and my friends to try to save the lives of at least some innocent unborn children and to offer help to their mothers. Now he had brought me to Africa to try to help better the lives of at least some Togolese. But he had something far more in mind. He wants every human life to be respected, and he wants all people to live under conditions that are decent and worthy of their human dignity. But he also wants our lives to open up to something infinitely more than what is possible here on earth. He sent his Son to inaugurate a kingdom where, not only all sin and suffering will be eliminated and all human goods will be found in their fullness, but also where we, his adopted children, will share fully in his own divine life.

Was I being called to follow Jesus in helping people to live for that kingdom, and eventually enter into it? Now I did begin to think about the priesthood, but it seemed best to return home before making any decision.

A Friend for Life

Shortly before I left Togo, I asked my friend the catechist where I could find a good priest I could speak with—not about a possible vocation to the priesthood, but about a priest who was giving a bad example and the effects it was having on people. The catechist recommended a young Togolese priest named Philippe Kpodzro, who was the headmaster of a boys' high school in Atakpamé, a town about fifteen miles away. I knocked on his door one day with no appointment.

Africans are generally gracious to strangers, and he was particularly so with me. He couldn't do anything directly about the bad situation, but was moved that a young American cared enough about the good of the Church to seek him out, and we hit it off immediately. It was the beginning of a friendship that has lasted thirty-five years. I have thought often about how the Lord used a scandalous situation to set the course of my life. If no bad example had been given, or if I had not been guided to Philippe Kpodzro to talk with him about it, the rest of my life would have been very different.

Reading a newspaper soon after returning to the U.S., I found a story about a Togolese priest being ordained bishop of Atakpamé. The ordination Mass was interrupted by soldiers who entered the cathedral and broke all the windows. The new bishop was Philippe Kpodzro! Years later he told me the full story. It was not a general persecution of the Church, but the president of Togo had been convinced that he should be the one to name the new bishop and had been persuaded to support a different candidate. Furious when his choice was rejected, he sent the soldiers. But the ordination had already taken place, and Bishop Kpodzro escaped safely out a back door of the cathedral. Although he remained in Togo, he was exiled from his diocese for four years—with a bounty on his head should he try to return—before the government at last allowed him to take up his episcopal ministry.

I entered Mount St. Mary's Seminary in Emmitsburg, Maryland, in 1976, to study for the Archdiocese of Washington, D.C. The four years until ordination to the priesthood passed quickly. While in the seminary, I often thought about Africa. But the conviction that I ought to return there as a missionary did not come until some years later. For one thing, I felt at the time an obligation to the pro-life movement. Some friends and I helped initiate Seminarians for Life, based at Mount St. Mary's. We sent out a newsletter to other seminaries around the country, organized workshops, and encouraged participation in the March for Life held each year in Washington on the anniversary of *Roe v. Wade*.

Within a few months after my priestly ordination in May of 1980, I was asked by Archbishop James Hickey to serve as pro-life coordinator for the Archdiocese of Washington, in addition to my parish duties. That was not easy for a lot of reasons, but with God's grace and the help of some great people, we started several crisis pregnancy centers and undertook some educational and advocacy activities.

Africa remained in my heart, though, and by 1985, the longing to return to Togo became profound. I had visited my Peace Corps village in 1981, and had stayed in touch over the years with Bishop Kpodzro. We had talked about the possibility of my returning one day. When I told him how my desire had deepened, he invited me to seek permission for temporary service in his diocese, where there was a grave shortage of priests. After much prayer I put my request to Archbishop Hickey.

A Different Kind of Mission

He had other ideas. Understandably concerned about the rapid influx of Spanish-speaking immigrants to the Washington area, he decided to send me and another priest to Latin America for a year of language and cultural studies as preparation to serve Hispanics. This was a deep disappointment to me, but not at all because of the new assignment itself, which I at once realized could be both pastorally fruitful and enriching for me personally. Rather, it was because I knew that my longing to go to Togo was for priestly service that the Church encouraged in the strongest possible language in its statements on the missions. I also foresaw that my desire was not likely to go away. I knew I couldn't make it go away, and now I wasn't sure what I should "do" with it. I had a lot to learn about patience.

All I could think to do was to ask our Lord for the grace to throw myself as completely into Hispanic ministry as if I had no desire to return to Africa. I suspect he smiled at that prayer. He certainly answered it, and then some. Hispanics are a wonderful people, and they gave me much more than I gave them. After the year in Latin America, mostly in the Dominican Republic and Colombia but with visits to many other countries, I was blessed with a spiritually rewarding ministry with Hispanics for sixteen unforgettable years, from 1986–2002.

The last nine of those years at St. Martin's Church in Gaithersburg, Maryland, were particularly fruitful. Three Sunday

Masses in Spanish were added during my time there, and participation in the religious education program for Hispanic children increased from one hundred to nine hundred. In God's wise plan, St. Martin's would eventually be a "sister" parish to my parish here in Togo, and would provide invaluable support for the mission.

There was enough to do in Hispanic ministry for more than a lifetime. Yet during all those years, the attraction to the African missions never left me. I had a deep sense that some very different chapters were yet to be written in my vocation story. My spiritual director encouraged me to keep seeking God's will and helped me to think things through.

In God's Time, Not Mine

The door finally opened in 2001 when I renewed my request to the new Archbishop of Washington, Theodore McCarrick. In his breezy way, he said sure, I could go to the African missions, but I would need to wait a year so that he could find someone for St. Martin's. It seemed that my long wait was almost over.

Little did I know that it would be not one but five more years—years that, as I look back on them, are now a blur. A freak knee injury led to a series of five failed operations—each of which, I was assured beforehand, had a high likelihood of success. A sixth surgery was successful enough to allow me to walk with a cane. If I don't overdo it, I can carry out a reasonably normal, though somewhat physically limited, ministry.

Every time an operation didn't work, I would call Togo to give then Archbishop Kpodzro (in 1992 he had been named

Archbishop of Lomé, the capital) the news that there would be yet another delay in my arrival. Each time I expected him to say, well, maybe your coming isn't God's will. But he always said the opposite: that he really thought I would come in God's good time, and that I should be patient. We agreed that we had both learned to be "experts in the art of waiting"—he while in exile from his first diocese and I during my long delay in beginning missionary service. *"Per crucem ad lucem,"* he would say to me: "Through the cross to the light."

I finally arrived here in Togo in 2006, the first American-born missionary ever to serve in this small French-speaking country. The only requests I made of Archbishop Kpodzro were that the new mission parish where I was to be the founding pastor would be in a rural area rather than the capital, and that it would be named Our Lady of Guadalupe.

That's because I wanted to bring the best of America with me—and without a doubt, Our Lady of Guadalupe is that. After all, she was given the title "Empress of the Americas" by Pope Pius XII and "Mother of the Americas" by Pope John XXIII. I wanted the graces Mary would obtain for her new mission parish here to be doubled, and half of them sent back home to be poured out upon the Hispanics and all the others I had served, especially at St. Martin's.

Since Our Lady of Guadalupe is also recognized more and more as the patroness of the pro-life movement, I wanted to remain spiritually joined through her to that great cause as well. And since it was Mary who obtained the greatest miracle of evangelization in the history of the Catholic Church, with nine million baptisms in the ten years following her apparition at Guadalupe in 1531,

I wanted her to be at the heart of the work of the mission, as we seek to bring the good news of her son Jesus to three dozen villages.

Already the mission has been abundantly blessed. Certainly in terms of construction, in a poor area where the Church had essentially no infrastructure, progress has been remarkable: There now are a rectory, a convent where three Togolese sisters have taken up residence, a medical clinic, schools and chapels in several villages, and of course, wells.

But the Church is being built up first and foremost in the hearts of the people. That task here in Togo is so enormous that St. Paul's question about missionary work—"Who is qualified for this?" (2 Corinthians 2:16)—readily answers itself. We priests know that, like Paul, we work from weakness, not from strength, and that the only way forward is to deepen our trust in Christ, to whom we were configured on the day of our ordination and into whose likeness we must grow more and more each day.

It has been rightly said that a missionary should work himself out of his job. As priestly ordinations for the Archdiocese of Lomé slowly increase, I know that an important part of my work is to prepare the way as well as I can for a Togolese priest to eventually take my place as pastor of this parish. How many years from now that will be, I can't say. I have learned that the future truly is in God's hands. For now, I can only praise him for bringing me here, and echo Mary's exultant cry: "The Almighty has done great things for me, and holy is his name!" (Luke 1:49).

For information on the progress of the mission parish of Our Lady of Guadalupe in Togo, including e-mail photo reports from Fr. Ryan, go to www.togomissionparish.org.

Chapter 30

Letter of His Holiness Pope Benedict XVI Proclaiming a Year for Priests

Dear Brother Priests,

On the forthcoming Solemnity of the Most Sacred Heart of Jesus, Friday, June 19, 2009—a day traditionally devoted to prayer for the sanctification of the clergy, I have decided to inaugurate a "Year for Priests" in celebration of the 150th anniversary of the *"dies natalis"* of John Mary Vianney, the patron saint of parish priests worldwide.[1] This Year, meant to deepen the commitment of all priests to interior renewal for the sake of a stronger and more incisive witness to the gospel in today's world, will conclude on the same Solemnity in 2010. *"The priesthood is the love of the heart of Jesus,"* the saintly Curé of Ars would often say.[2] This touching expression makes us reflect, first of all, with heartfelt gratitude on the immense gift which priests represent, not only for the Church, but also for humanity itself. I think of all those priests who quietly present Christ's words and actions each day to the faithful and to the whole world, striving to be one with the Lord in their thoughts and their will, their sentiments and their style of life. How can I not pay tribute to their apostolic labors, their tireless and hidden service, their universal charity? And how can I not praise the courageous fidelity of so many priests who, even amid difficulties and incomprehension, remain faithful to their vocation as "friends of Christ," whom he has called by name, chosen and sent?

I still treasure the memory of the first parish priest at whose side I exercised my ministry as a young priest: He left me an example of unreserved devotion to his pastoral duties, even to meeting his own death in the act of bringing viaticum to a gravely ill person. I also recall the countless confreres whom I have met and continue to meet, not least in my pastoral visits to different countries: men generously dedicated to the daily exercise of their priestly ministry. Yet the expression of St. John Mary also makes us think of Christ's pierced heart and the crown of thorns which surrounds it. I also think, therefore, of the countless situations of suffering endured by many priests, either because they themselves share in the manifold human experience of pain or because they encounter misunderstanding from the very persons to whom they minister. How can we not also think of all those priests who are offended in their dignity, obstructed in their mission, and persecuted, even at times to offering the supreme testimony of their own blood?

There are also, sad to say, situations which can never be sufficiently deplored where the Church herself suffers as a consequence of infidelity on the part of some of her ministers. Then it is the world which finds grounds for scandal and rejection. What is most helpful to the Church in such cases is not only a frank and complete acknowledgment of the weaknesses of her ministers, but also a joyful and renewed realization of the greatness of God's gift, embodied in the splendid example of generous pastors, religious on fire with love for God and for souls, and insightful, patient spiritual guides. Here the teaching and example of St. John Mary Vianney can serve as a significant point of reference for us all. The Curé of Ars was very humble, yet as a priest he was conscious of being an immense gift to his people: "A good shepherd, a pastor after God's heart, is the greatest treasure which the good Lord can grant to a parish, and one of the most precious gifts of divine mercy."[3] He spoke of the priesthood as if incapable of fathoming the grandeur of the *gift* and *task* entrusted to a human creature: "O, how great is the priest! . . . If he realized what he is, he would die. . . . God obeys him: he utters a few words and the Lord descends from heaven at his voice, to be contained within a small host. . . . "[4] Explaining to his parishioners the importance of the sacraments, he would say:

Without the Sacrament of Holy Orders, we would not have the Lord. Who put him there in that tabernacle? The priest. Who welcomed your soul at the beginning of your life? The priest. Who feeds your soul and gives it strength for its journey? The priest. Who will prepare it to appear before God, bathing it one last time in the blood of Jesus Christ? The priest, always the priest. And if this soul should happen to die [as a result of sin], who will raise it up, who will restore its calm and peace? Again, the priest . . . After God, the priest is everything! . . . Only in heaven will he fully realize what he is.[5]

These words, welling up from the priestly heart of the holy pastor, might sound excessive. Yet they reveal the high esteem in which he held the sacrament of the priesthood. He seemed overwhelmed by a boundless sense of responsibility:

Were we to fully realize what a priest is on earth, we would die: not of fright, but of love. . . . Without the priest, the passion and death of our Lord would be of no avail. It is the priest who continues the work of redemption on earth. . . . What use would be a house filled with gold, were there no one to open its door? The priest holds the key to the treasures of heaven: it is he who opens the door; he is the steward of the good Lord; the administrator of his goods. . . . Leave a parish for twenty years without a priest, and they will end by worshiping the beasts there. . . . The priest is not a priest for himself, he is a priest for you.[6]

He arrived in Ars, a village of 230 souls, warned by his bishop beforehand that there he would find religious practice in a sorry state: "There is little love of God in that parish; you will be the one to put it there." As a result, he was deeply aware that he needed to go there to embody Christ's presence and to bear witness to his saving mercy: "[Lord,] grant me the conversion of my parish; I am willing to suffer whatever you wish, for my entire life!": with this prayer he entered upon his mission.[7] The Curé devoted himself completely to his parish's conversion, setting before all else the Christian education of the people in his care.

Dear brother priests, let us ask the Lord Jesus for the grace to learn for ourselves something of the pastoral plan of St. John Mary Vianney! The first thing we need to learn is the complete identification of the man with his ministry. In Jesus, person and mission tend to coincide: All Christ's saving activity was, and is, an expression of his "filial consciousness," which from all eternity stands before the Father in an attitude of loving submission to his will. In a humble yet genuine way, every priest must aim for a similar identification. Certainly this is not to forget that the efficacy of the ministry is independent of the holiness of the minister; but neither can we overlook the extraordinary fruitfulness of the encounter between the ministry's objective holiness and the subjective holiness of the minister. The Curé of Ars immediately set about this patient and humble task of harmonizing his life as a minister with the holiness of the ministry he had received, by deciding to *"live,"* physically, in his parish church. As his first biographer tells us: "Upon his arrival, he chose the church as his home. He entered the church before dawn and did not leave it until after the evening Angelus. There he was to be sought whenever needed."[8]

The pious excess of his devout biographer should not blind us to the fact that the Curé also knew how to "live" actively within the entire territory of his parish: He regularly visited the sick and families; organized popular missions and patronal feasts; collected and managed funds for charitable and missionary works; embellished and furnished his parish church; cared for the orphans and teachers of the *"Providence"* (an institute he founded); provided for the education of children; founded confraternities and enlisted laypersons to work at his side.

His example naturally leads me to point out that there are sectors of cooperation which need to be opened ever more fully to the lay faithful. Priests and laity together make up the one priestly people,[9] and in virtue of their ministry, priests live in the midst of the lay faithful, "that they may lead everyone to the unity of charity, 'loving one another with mutual affection; and outdoing one another in sharing honor'" (see Romans 12:10).[10] Here we ought to recall the Second Vatican Council's hearty encouragement to priests "to be sincere in their appreciation and promotion of the dignity of the laity and of the special role they have to play in the

Church's mission. . . . They should be willing to listen to laypeople, give brotherly consideration to their wishes, and acknowledge their experience and competence in the different fields of human activity. In this way they will be able together with them to discern the signs of the times."[11]

St. John Mary Vianney taught his parishioners primarily by the witness of his life. It was from his example that they learned to pray, halting frequently before the tabernacle for a visit to Jesus in the Blessed Sacrament.[12] "One need not say much to pray well," the Curé explained to them. "We know that Jesus is there in the tabernacle: let us open our hearts to him, let us rejoice in his sacred presence. That is the best prayer."[13] And he would urge them: "Come to communion, my brothers and sisters, come to Jesus. Come to live from him in order to live with him. . . ."[14] "Of course you are not worthy of him, but *you need him!*"[15] This way of educating the faithful *to the Eucharistic presence and to communion* proved most effective when they saw him celebrate the Holy Sacrifice of the Mass. Those present said that "it was not possible to find a finer example of worship. . . . He gazed upon the Host with immense love."[16] "All good works, taken together, do not equal the sacrifice of the Mass," he would say, "since they are human works, while the Holy Mass is the work of God."[17] He was convinced that the fervor of a priest's life depended entirely upon the Mass: "The reason why a priest is lax is that he does not pay attention to the Mass! My God, how we ought to pity a priest who celebrates as if he were engaged in something routine!"[18] He was accustomed, when celebrating, also to offer his own life in sacrifice: "What a good thing it is for a priest each morning to offer himself to God in sacrifice!"[19]

This deep personal identification with the sacrifice of the cross led him—by a sole inward movement—from the altar to the confessional. Priests ought never to be resigned to empty confessionals or the apparent indifference of the faithful to this sacrament. In France, at the time of the Curé of Ars, confession was no more easy or frequent than in our own day, since the upheaval caused by the revolution had long inhibited the practice of religion. Yet he sought in every way, by his preaching and his powers of persuasion, to help his parishioners to rediscover the meaning and beauty of the Sacrament of Penance, presenting it as an inherent demand of the Eucharistic presence. He thus created a *"virtuous" circle.* By spending long hours in church before the tabernacle, he inspired the faithful to imitate him by coming to visit Jesus with the knowledge that their parish priest would be there, ready to listen and offer forgiveness. Later, the growing numbers of penitents from all over France would keep him in the confessional for up to sixteen hours a day. It was said that Ars had become "a great hospital of souls."[20] His first biographer relates that "the grace he obtained [for the conversion of sinners] was so powerful that it would pursue them, not leaving them a moment of peace!"[21] The saintly Curé reflected something of the same idea when he said, "It is not the sinner who returns to God to beg his forgiveness, but God himself who runs after the sinner and makes him return to him."[22] "This good Savior is so filled with love that he seeks us everywhere."[23] We priests should feel that the following words, which he put on the lips of Christ, are meant for each of us personally: "I will charge my ministers to proclaim to sinners that I am ever ready to welcome them, that my mercy is infinite."[24] From St. John Mary Vianney we can learn to put our unfailing trust in the Sacrament of Penance, to set it once more at the center of our pastoral concerns, and to take up the "dialogue of salvation" which it entails.

The Curé of Ars dealt with different penitents in different ways. Those who came to his confessional drawn by a deep and humble longing for God's forgiveness found in him the encouragement to plunge into the "flood of divine mercy," which sweeps everything away by its vehemence. If someone was troubled by the thought of his own frailty and inconstancy, and fearful of sinning again, the Curé would unveil the mystery of God's love in these beautiful and touching words: "The good Lord knows everything. Even before you confess, he already knows that you will sin again, yet he still forgives you. How great is the love of our God: he *even forces himself to forget the future*, so that he can grant us his forgiveness!"[25] But to those who made a lukewarm and rather indifferent confession of sin, he clearly demonstrated by his own tears of pain how "abominable" this attitude was: "I weep because you don't weep,"[26] he would say. "If only the Lord were not so good! *But he is so good!* One would have to be a brute to treat so good a Father this way!"[27] He awakened repentance in the hearts of the lukewarm by forcing them to see God's own pain at their sins reflected in the face of the priest who was their confessor. To those who, on the other hand, came to him already desiring of and suited to a deeper spiritual life, he flung open the abyss of God's love, explaining the untold beauty of living in union with him and dwelling in his presence: "Everything in God's sight, everything with God, everything to please God . . . How beautiful it is!"[28] And he taught them to pray: "My God, grant me the grace to love you as much as I possibly can."[29] . . .

In today's world, as in the troubled times of the Curé of Ars, the lives and activity of priests need to be distinguished by *a determined witness to the gospel*. As Pope Paul VI rightly noted, "Modern man listens more willingly to witnesses than to teachers, and if he does listen to teachers, it is because they are witnesses."[30] Lest we experience existential emptiness and the effectiveness of our ministry be compromised, we need to ask ourselves ever anew: "Are we truly pervaded by the word of God? Is that word truly the nourishment we live by, even more than bread and the things of this world? Do we really know that word? Do we love it? Are we deeply engaged with this word to the point that it really leaves a mark on our lives and shapes our thinking?"[31] Just as Jesus called the Twelve to be with him (cf. Mark 3:14), and only later sent them forth to preach, so too in our days priests are called to assimilate that "new style of life" which was inaugurated by the Lord Jesus and taken up by the Apostles.[32]

It was complete commitment to this "new style of life" which marked the priestly ministry of the Curé of Ars. Pope John XXIII, in his encyclical letter *Sacerdotii Nostri Primordia*, published in 1959 on the first centennial of the death of St. John Mary Vianney, presented his asceticism with special reference to the "three evangelical counsels" which the pope considered necessary also for diocesan priests: "even though priests are not bound to embrace these evangelical counsels by virtue of the clerical state, these counsels nonetheless offer them, as they do all the faithful, the surest road to the desired goal of Christian perfection."[33]

The Curé of Ars lived the "evangelical counsels" in a way suited to his priestly state. His *poverty* was not the poverty of a religious or a monk, but that proper to a priest: While managing much money (since well-to-do pilgrims naturally took an interest in his charitable works), he realized that everything had been donated to his church, his poor, his orphans, the girls of his *Providence*,[34] his families of modest means. Consequently, he "was rich in giving to others and very poor for himself."[35] As he would explain: "My secret is simple: give everything away; hold nothing back."[36] When he lacked money, he would say amiably to the poor who knocked at his door: "Today I'm poor just like you, I'm one of you."[37] At the end of his life, he could say with absolute tranquility: "I no longer have anything. The good Lord can call me whenever he wants!"[38]

His *chastity*, too, was that demanded of a priest for his ministry. It could be said that it was a chastity suited to one who must daily touch the Eucharist, who contemplates it blissfully and with that same bliss offers it to his flock. It was said of him that "he radiated chastity"; the faithful would see this when he turned and gazed at the tabernacle with loving eyes."[39]

Finally, St. John Mary Vianney's *obedience* found full embodiment in his conscientious fidelity to the daily demands of his ministry. We know how he was tormented by the thought of his inadequacy for parish ministry and by a desire to flee "in order to bewail his poor life, in solitude."[40] Only obedience and a thirst for souls convinced him to remain at his post. As he explained to himself and his flock: "There are no two good ways of serving God. There is only one: serve him as he desires to be served."[41] He considered this the golden rule for a life of obedience: "Do only what can be offered to the good Lord."[42]

In this context of a spirituality nourished by the practice of the evangelical counsels, I would like to invite all priests, during this

Year dedicated to them, to welcome the new springtime which the Spirit is now bringing about in the Church, not least through the ecclesial movements and the new communities. "In his gifts the Spirit is multifaceted . . . He breathes where he wills. He does so unexpectedly, in unexpected places, and in ways previously unheard of . . . but he also shows us that he works with a view to the one body and in the unity of the one body."[43] In this regard, the statement of the decree *Presbyterorum Ordinis* continues to be timely: "While testing the spirits to discover if they be of God, priests must discover with faith, recognize with joy, and foster diligently the many and varied charismatic gifts of the laity, whether these be of a humble or more exalted kind."[44] These gifts, which awaken in many people the desire for a deeper spiritual life, can benefit not only the lay faithful but the clergy as well. The communion between ordained and charismatic ministries can provide "a helpful impulse to a renewed commitment by the Church in proclaiming and bearing witness to the Gospel of hope and charity in every corner of the world."[45]

I would also like to add, echoing the apostolic exhortation *Pastores Dabo Vobis* of Pope John Paul II, that the ordained ministry has a radical *"communitarian form"* and can be exercised only in the communion of priests with their bishop.[46] This communion between priests and their bishop, grounded in the Sacrament of Holy Orders and made manifest in Eucharistic concelebration, needs to be translated into various concrete expressions of an effective and affective priestly fraternity.[47] Only thus will priests be able to live fully the gift of celibacy and build thriving Christian communities in which the miracles which accompanied the first preaching of the gospel can be repeated. . . .

The Pauline Year now coming to its close invites us also to look to the Apostle of the Gentiles, who represents a splendid example of a priest entirely devoted to his ministry. "The love of Christ urges us on," he wrote, "because we are convinced that one has died for all; therefore all have died" (2 Corinthians 5:14). And he adds: "He died for all, so that those who live might live no longer for themselves, but for him who died and was raised for them" (5:15). Could a finer program be proposed to any priest resolved to advance along the path of Christian perfection? . . .

To the Most Holy Virgin I entrust this Year for Priests. I ask her to awaken in the heart of every priest a generous and renewed commitment to the ideal of complete self-oblation to Christ and the Church which inspired the thoughts and actions of the saintly Curé of Ars. It was his fervent prayer life and his impassioned love of Christ Crucified that enabled John Mary Vianney to grow daily in his total self-oblation to God and the Church. May his example lead all priests to offer that witness of unity with their bishop, with one another, and with the lay faithful, which today, as ever, is so necessary. Despite all the evil present in our world, the words which Christ spoke to his apostles in the upper room continue to inspire us: "In the world you have tribulation; but take courage, I have overcome the world" (John 16:33). Our faith in the Divine Master gives us the strength to look to the future with confidence. Dear priests, Christ is counting on you. In the footsteps of the Curé of Ars, let yourselves be enthralled by him. In this way you too will be, for the world in our time, heralds of hope, reconciliation, and peace!

From the Vatican, 16 June 2009.

1. He was proclaimed as such by Pope Pius XI in 1929.

2. *"Le Sacerdoce, c'est l'amour du cœur de Jésus"* (in *Le curé d'Ars. Sa pensée – Son cœur.* Présentés par l'Abbé Bernard Nodet, éd. Xavier Mappus, Foi Vivante, 1966, p. 98). Hereafter: *Nodet.* The expression is also quoted in the *Catechism of the Catholic Church*, No. 1589.

3. Nodet, p. 101.

4. Ibid., p. 97.

5. Ibid., pp. 98-99.

6. Ibid., pp. 98-100.

7. Ibid., p. 183.

8. Monnin, A., *Il Curato d'Ars. Vita di Gian.Battista-Maria Vianney*, vol. I, ed. Marietti, Turin, 1870, p. 122.

9. Cf. *Lumen Gentium*, 10.

10. *Presbyterorum Ordinis*, 9.

11. Ibid.

12. "Contemplation is a gaze of faith, fixed on Jesus. 'I look at him and he looks at me': this is what a certain peasant of Ars used to say to his holy Curé about his prayer before the tabernacle" (*Catechism of the Catholic Church*, No. 2715).

13. Nodet, p. 85.

14. Ibid., p. 114.

15. Ibid., p. 119.

16. Monnin, pp. 430ff.

17. Nodet, p. 105.

18. Ibid.

19. Ibid., p. 104.

20. Monnin, p. 293.

21. Ibid., II, p. 10.

22. Nodet, p. 128.

23. Ibid., p. 50.

24. Ibid., p. 131.

25. Ibid., p. 130.

26. Ibid., p. 27.

27. Ibid., p. 139.

28. Ibid., p. 28.

29. Ibid., p. 77.

30. *Evangelii Nuntiandi*, 41.

31. Benedict XVI, *Homily at the Chrism Mass*, 9 April 2009.

32. Cf. Benedict XVI, *Address to the Plenary Assembly of the Congregation for the Clergy*, 16 March 2009.

33. *Sacerdotii Nostri Primordia, 12*

34. The name given to the house where more than sixty abandoned girls were taken in and educated. To maintain this house, he would do anything: *"J'ai fait tous les commerces imaginables,"* he would say with a smile (Nodet, p. 214).

35. Nodet, p. 216.

36. Ibid., p. 215.

37. Ibid., p. 216.

38. Ibid., p. 214.

39. Cf. ibid., p. 112.

40. Cf. ibid., pp. 82-84; 102-103.

41. Ibid., p. 75.

42. Ibid., p. 76.

43. Benedict XVI, *Homily for the Vigil of Pentecost*, 3 June 2006.

44. *Presbyterorum Ordinis*, 9.

45. Benedict XVI, *Address to Bishop-Friends of the Focolare Movement and the Sant'Egidio Community*, 8 February 2007.

46. Cf. No. 17.

47. Cf. John Paul II, Apostolic Exhortation *Pastores Dabo Vobis*, 74.

ACKNOWLEDGMENTS

The People's Prayer for Priests taken from the U.S. Conference of Catholic Bishops' Web site on the Year for Priests. Used with permission.

Excerpt of Cardinal Joseph Bernardin's homily, "I Am Joseph, Your Brother," were reprinted with permission of the Archdiocese of Chicago's Joseph Cardinal Bernardin Archives and Records Center.

Article by Fr. John Dear, SJ, adapted from *A Persistent Peace: One Man's Struggle for a Nonviolent World* (Loyola Press, 2008). Reprinted with permission of Loyola Press. To order copies, call 1-800-621-1008 or go to www.loyolapress.com.

"In Praise of Horizontal Prayer" by Fr. Frank Moan, SJ, was reprinted from *America* magazine, February 14, 2005 edition, with permission of America Press, Inc. "The Grass is Greeen Everywhere" by Fr. James Martin, SJ, was reprinted from *America* magazine, September 26, 2000 edition, with permission of America Press, Inc. All rights reserved. For subscription information, call 1-800-627-9533 or visit www.americamagazine.org.

Letter of His Holiness Pope Benedict XVI Proclaiming a Year for Priests was reprinted with permission of Libreria Editrice Vaticana. © Libreria Editrice Vaticana. Used with permission. All rights reserved.

the WORD
among us®
The Spirit of Catholic Living

T his book was published by The Word Among Us. For nearly thirty years,
The Word Among Us has been answering the call of the Second Vatican
Council to help Catholic laypeople encounter Christ in the Scriptures—a
call reiterated recently by Pope Benedict XVI and a Synod of Bishops.

The name of our company comes from the prologue to the Gospel of John
and reflects the vision and purpose of all of our publications: to be an instrument of the Spirit, whose desire is to manifest Jesus' presence in and to the
children of God. In this way, we hope to contribute to the church's ongoing mission of proclaiming the gospel to the world and growing ever more
deeply in our love for the Lord.

Our monthly devotional magazine, *The Word Among Us*, features
meditations on the daily and Sunday Mass readings, and currently reaches
more than one million Catholics in North America each year and another
500,000 Catholics in 100 countries. Our press division has published nearly
180 books and Bible studies over the past ten years.

To learn more about who we are and what we publish, log on to our Web
site at **www.wau.org**. There you will find a variety of Catholic resources
that will help you grow in your faith.

Embrace His Word, Listen to God . . .

www.wau.org